The Enquiring
University Teacher

SRHE and Open University Press Imprint
General Editor: Heather Eggins

Published by SRHE and
Open University Press
Celtic Court
22 Ballmoor
Buckingham
MK18 1XW

email enquiries@openup.co.uk
world wide web: http://www.openup.co.uk

and 325 Chestnut Street
Philadelphia, PA19106, USA

First published 2000

A catalogue record of this book is available from the British Library

ISBN 0 335 20507 0 (pbk)   0 335 20508 9 (hbk)

Library of Congress Cataloging-in-Publication Data
Rowland, Stephen.
     The enquiring university teacher / by Stephen Rowland.
        p.   cm.
     Includes bibliographical references and index.
     ISBN 0–335–20508–9 (hb) — ISBN 0–335–20507–0 (pb)
     1. College teaching. 2. Research. I. Title.

LB2331.R69   2000
378.1'2—dc21   99–050127

Typeset by Graphicraft Limited, Hong Kong
Printed in Great Britain by St Edmundsbury Press, Bury St Edmunds, Suffolk

The Enquiring
University Teacher

Stephen Rowland, 1947-

The Society for Research into Higher Education
& Open University Press

Contents

Acknowledgements

I would like to thank those colleagues who were also my students, co-researchers, informants and subjects in this study. They will not know how much I have learned from them. In particular Bob Booth, Robert Edyvean, Russell Hand, Lin Mellor, John Stratford, Robin Walters and Ceri Williams play a part in this story.

I also want to thank Len Barton for joining with me in setting up, teaching and writing about the course that provided the original stimulus for this book; Jon Nixon for taking it further with me; and Alan Skelton for collaborating in every aspect of its recent development and, in particular, for taking over my own teaching responsibilities so that I could have the time to write this book.

This enquiry would not have been possible without the support of the Department of Educational Studies at Sheffield University, in which I have worked for 14 years and have found the intellectual space to pursue my ideas. Regrettably, this has become a rare privilege, rather than a right, in academic life.

Gillie Bolton's contribution is unusual. She has read and commented on everything written here, and at times even knew what I wanted to write before I did. Like a tangle of arms and legs, I am sometimes unable to distinguish her ideas and insights from my own.

I would like to acknowledge the journals in which I have published work that has been further developed in some of the chapters here. They are:

Chapter 2: (1996) Relationships between teaching and research, *Teaching in Higher Education*, 1(1): 7–20.

Chapter 3 (with Barton, L.): (1994) Making things difficult: developing a research approach to teaching in Higher Education, *Studies in Higher Education*, 19(3): 367–74.

Chapter 4: (1999) A pedagogical theory for university lecturers, *Studies in Higher Education*, 24(3): 303–14.

Chapter 6: (1997) A lovers' guide to university teaching?, *Educational Action Research*, 5(2): 243–55.

Chapter 7: (1997) Reflections upon a story, *Journal of Academic Development*, 3(2): 19–35.

1

Introduction to the Enquiry

Exploring difference

'You've been making things difficult for me, you have,' Chris said on entering my office.

I know Chris enjoys a bit of gentle provocation, but this is not a good start, I thought.

'Since I joined this group I've been unable to teach the way I used to,' he continued.

Chris was an experienced lecturer in accountancy and financial management. In his early forties, he had recently joined a group of a dozen academics from different disciplines, levels of experience and age, who were piloting a new Masters course in learning and teaching for staff at his university. As director of this pilot course I was somewhat disturbed by his opening comment in what was supposed to be a tutorial for his work on the course. Had the course so far really led to him feeling disempowered?

As the conversation proceeded, however, he began to make clear that his feeling of being unable to teach as he had done was also the beginning of a process that he called 'enlightenment'. While on the one hand this process of change often felt uncomfortable, unfamiliar and unpredictable, on the other, it led to exciting new possibilities for his work with students now that he questioned many of the assumptions upon which his teaching had been based.

At a time when most of us in higher education are increasingly being held to account for the quality of our teaching, I want, in this book, to give emphasis to the unpredictable and exploratory nature of learning (and learning about teaching). Of course we should be held to account for our teaching. But there is a danger that amid the concerns for quality assurance, training of university teachers and raising of standards, we forget an important aspect of the most valuable learning: we can never be quite sure where it will lead. This is why Chris felt uneasy and, at the same time, excited. He knew that the development of his teaching was inevitably exploratory: it involved him in leaving behind old certainties just as much as opening up new possibilities.

A sense of personal exploration will be a recurrent theme in this book. As the title suggests it is an enquiry, or research. Like many research endeavours it is incomplete and raises as many new questions as it answers old ones. It investigates a number of related themes arising from my work, which are, I hope, of interest to anyone who, like me, teaches, researches, writes and, most importantly, attempts to learn, in a university setting. Its focus is on our learning as university teachers attempting to improve our teaching. As the philosopher Heidegger once put it, only the teacher 'who can truly learn – and only as long as they can do it – can truly teach' (Heiddegger 1978: 251).

The context of most of this activity has been my work alongside other academics, who, like the group of people with whom Chris worked on his pilot Masters course, come from a wide range of backgrounds but share an interest in teaching and learning.

This book is also written *for* people from across this range of disciplinary backgrounds and levels of experience. This presents me with my initial problem and the second recurrent theme of the book: how can we speak to each other, and learn from each other, across the divides between the disciplines and roles that we take on? At a practical level, what (and how) can a dentist learn from a historian about teaching and learning? At a more theoretical or philosophical level, what assumptions about what it means to 'know' something underlie teaching in dentistry and history and how do they differ?

In the UK, in spite of a development over more than 45 years to increase the opportunities for students to cooperate with specialists from disciplines other than their own (Beard and Hartley 1984: 4), and current policy documents that reflect a similar concern for multidisciplinary work (National Committee of Inquiry into Higher Education (NCIHE) 1997), academics work in an increasingly fragmented environment.

This fragmentation relates, however, not only to the differentiation between disciplines themselves, but to the differentiation between teaching and research, academics and managers, teachers and students, and academics and academic developers. Indeed, the idea of *uno voce* (one voice) or universality, which the etymology of the word 'university' might seem to suggest, is far removed from the experience of many of us who work in these institutions. It is an old cliché that the only thing that academics share is a joint concern to find a car parking space.

It is against this experience of a fragmented work setting that we should understand the institutional demands for standardization, mission statements, quality audit, and the rest of the paraphernalia aimed at creating order and control in the face of chaotic and disconnected experience.

In attempting to engage questions about learning with an audience from such widely different ways of thinking, with different ways of expressing their ideas, and with different interests, it is tempting to view teaching and learning as being *generic*. This is the common assumption that although university teachers are scholars of a particular subject, questions about teaching and learning are of a different order: that the teacher of dentistry and the teacher of history have much to learn about the nature of teaching and learning (and how to do it) that is independent of the subject. Starting from this premise, one of two different conclusions are often drawn.

The first is that teaching is primarily a practical activity; a craft that can be learnt through familiarity without undue intellectual or theoretical effort. According to this view, the academic's *intellectual* efforts should be directed towards research. Teaching is a *practical* activity, that they have to take part in, that may, or may not, be of interest. It follows from this that the development of university teaching is largely a matter of ensuring that academics take part in various programmes that ensure they gain the necessary familiarity and practice. In a university culture that traditionally values its intellectual contribution to society, it is not surprising that, according to this way of thinking, teaching is viewed as a somewhat menial and amateurish task compared to the real intellectual work of research (Booth 1998: 1). There is a danger, if we accept this view, that policies and institutions that promote initial compulsory 'teacher training' for university staff might merely serve to reinforce this prejudice, unless teaching is also seen to be intellectually exciting.

An alternative conclusion, to be drawn from the assumption that teaching is largely generic across different subject matters, is that questions of teaching and learning are the special concern of *educationalists* and educational researchers who develop educational theory. According to this way of thinking it seems unrealistic to expect an academic who is a historian or dentist also to be an educationalist, for the study of education is a different discipline, which requires a different way of thinking. It follows from this that the development of university teaching should be guided by specialist educationalists who theorize, conduct research and produce 'findings' about teaching and learning that can then be 'applied' by the non-educationalist academics in their discipline. This view of professional development underlies recent criticism of educational research in schooling in the UK, which, it alleges, largely fails to produce findings that are applied to classroom teaching (Department for Education and Employment (DfEE) 1998a; Tooley and Darby 1998).

The argument I shall develop through this book is sceptical of both of these conclusions and raises some questions about the premise upon which they are based – that teaching and learning are largely generic. While learning (and therefore teaching about) how to fill a tooth, or interpret a historical text, or investigate sub-atomic particles might have some interesting things in common, the *differences* between them might be even more revealing as we explore ways of developing our own teaching and learning. Indeed, it may be that dentists and historians tend to think differently by virtue of their different backgrounds and that they apply these different ways of thinking to their teaching. Our experience of working with mixed groups of lecturers suggests that they learn much from each other by drawing upon these differences, rather than by submerging them within the generic aspects of teaching.

The second theme of the book, then, is an attempt to address questions of teaching and learning by drawing upon the differences between academics from different subjects, and also upon the different roles we play, as researchers, learners, teachers and students. In the process, I hope to show how some of the distinctions we readily make – between teaching and research, and between students and teachers – might be less oppositional than is often assumed.

Is this book theoretical or practical?

Perhaps the most fundamental oppositional, or rather *dualistic*, relationship that underlies much thinking about teaching and learning is the relationship between theory and practice. The view that teaching is a practical activity that is (or rather, should be) based upon theory derived from specialist educational research is a view that comes from a particular conception about the relationship between theory and practice. According to this conception, theory provides us with a pure, idealized and abstract model, and practice is what actually happens. Good practice – in, say, teaching – is what takes place when what actually happens – our teaching – is as close as possible to the theory. Now this view of theory and practice might make sense as an everyday way of thinking about, say, Copernicus's theory about the planets revolving around the sun: the practice nicely fits the theory. But I think its value is extremely limited when it comes to thinking about teaching.

When Chris, whose comments opened this chapter, explained to me that he felt that things were now difficult because he could not teach as he used to, he was not saying that he now had a new 'educational theory' that he was struggling to apply. On the contrary, his uneasy excitement about his teaching was the result of having a complex of theories, half formed ideas, doubts and awareness of new possibilities, which had not occurred to him with his previous assumptions about his role as a teacher. In this uncertain state he would, of course, try out new ideas with his students, reflect upon his teaching and come to new understandings of his students. For example, at one stage, a few weeks after this visit to me, he decided to have his students meet for a group tutorial without the tutor. This led to a productive development among his students, who, he felt, gained a sense of responsibility for their learning and a decreased dependency upon their tutor. But in as much as Chris was a good teacher, it was not because he was following a 'good' educational theory; it was because he was thoughtful about what he was doing.

What I hope to do in this book is to show what such 'thoughtfulness' might be, how it might be developed and promoted and how it might give some intellectual life to our teaching. In the attempt to do this, the book will be very practical in one sense; it will draw heavily upon my own practice as a teacher and researcher in the field of 'teaching and learning in higher education'. In this way it may also suggest practices that others might wish to try out in order to make their teaching a more thoughtful and rewarding activity. But it is not a handbook on 'how to do it'; nor does it offer tips to be followed. With apologies to Graham Gibbs, who wrote an influential book called *53 Interesting Things to do in your Lectures* (Gibbs and Habeshaw 1987), and a number of other titles involving 53 practical suggestions, I am not tempted to call this book: *53 Interesting Ways to be an Enquiring Teacher*. It is, I hope, an invitation to explore rather than a recipe for success.

There is also a way in which this book is theoretical. It is an attempt to theorize – in the sense of systematically reflect upon – my practice as a university teacher and collaborator with other university teachers. In doing so it will articulate some principles and values that I believe might form a sound basis for developing university teaching. It will also, I hope, stimulate readers in the development of their own reflections and theories about their learning and teaching. It will not, however, attempt to provide a review of the range of theories that relate to teaching and learning in higher education. While I shall draw lightly upon my own eclectic interests and limited knowledge in philosophy, sociology, psychology, science and other disciplines, I shall not assume that the reader has any deep understanding of the theoretical resources that each has to offer such an enquiry. Nor will I assume any particular understanding of educational theory.

These brief comments about the book's theoretical or practical orientation beg a range of questions, which later chapters will address. Before I introduce some of these, however, there is another important issue, which is tied up with the question of whether this is primarily a practical or a theoretical book. Often this question is a reference to how the text demonstrates its relationship to other texts in the field: is this a scholarly work that positions itself in the field of the research literature? As I have suggested, I do not intend to do this. But there is one very general point I do wish to make about the relationship between this enquiry and existing texts about learning in higher education. I need to indicate this point at the beginning in order to clarify what kind of enquiry might be involved when we think about our practice as teachers. I shall illustrate it by referring to just two books. Although both books are by widely respected researchers and concern learning in higher education, familiarity with them is not important for my argument.

The first book is called *The Impact of Teaching on Learning Outcomes in Higher Education: A Literature Review* (Entwistle 1992). Although this book is not very recent nor quite contemporaneous with the second book I shall draw upon, it is a fairly wide ranging review of the literature that the author believes to relate to the subject of how teaching affects what students learn.

The second book, *Higher Education: A Critical Business* (Barnett 1997) develops the idea that higher education should have the outcome of helping students to 'reflect critically on knowledge but (they) also develop their powers of critical self-reflection and critical action' (back cover).

Both books are concerned, then, with the outcomes of higher education teaching: the first in general terms, and the second in relation to its critical purpose. One might expect, therefore, that these texts draw upon a similar field of literature.

In fact, this is very far from the case. Entwistle's book refers to texts from 132 primary authors and editors; Barnett's refers to 126. Apart from one writer who appears as an editor in one of the bibliographies and an author in the other, no other author or editor is referred to by both Barnett and Entwistle.

The only reasonable conclusion we can draw from this is that in spite of a surface appearance that both books might relate to the same field, in fact they have very different concerns. Such a conclusion must be pretty confusing to anyone who is wanting to study the field of teaching and learning in higher education. How can it be that two important texts both about learning in higher education should have so little in common?

The answer, I believe, is that when Barnett and Entwistle think about learning, they think about very different things. Barnett has described himself as a social philosopher (Barnett 1994: 1). He is therefore interested in how learning relates to the wider context of society (as a sociologist) and in analysing in some depth the concepts involved (as a philosopher). Entwistle, on the other hand, has a more psychological orientation and is interested in learning and teaching processes and how they influence each other.

Now I do not wish to discuss the relative merits of these works. I could easily have chosen other pairs of writers to make the same point. I do, however, as an introduction to the enquiry that this book will pursue, want to make just two salient observations.

First, the field of 'teaching and learning in higher education' is itself fragmented. There are major writers in the field who appear not to be speaking to one another. Earlier in this introduction I mentioned the fragmentation that characterizes academic work. What I have illustrated here is that this fragmentation occurs *within* the field of education as well as between the disciplines. Such fragmentation occurs within the social sciences and humanities generally, and increasingly in the natural sciences too. We can no longer assume to be able to carry out (or interested in carrying out) a dialogue about our work, even with colleagues who share our discipline. Indeed, in as much as this is the case, the very concept of a 'discipline' is brought into question. As knowledge has rapidly expanded, so the multitude of voices, discourses or special languages has increased, with the result that communication becomes more problematic and confined to increasingly narrow communities. My hope in this book is to be able to speak across the divides *within* the field of education, as well as between the different disciplines.

Second, if we want to develop ourselves as university teachers, which is my project for this book, we need to consider broader questions concerning, for example, the purpose of teaching, the values that might underlie it and the kind of academic community and the kind of society we are involved in creating, as *well* as the immediate questions of what to do with a group of students. To concentrate only on the former broader questions may amount to little more than armchair philosophy. If we concentrate only on the latter we may become technically competent teachers. In order to be *professional* teachers, however, we need to understand how our practice relates to wider social values and purposes. Without this, our teaching may merely serve purposes that are beyond our ken, which may be quite at odds with our own moral values, and which may merely reflect current fads and fashions in teaching. Such an approach to our teaching would be uncritical: our learning about it would be only a surface learning, like that of the undergraduate student who learns how to perform experiments without understanding their wider significance.

Much that is written and understood about teaching in higher education, and the way that its development is organized, reflects a lack of connection between questions about how to teach and the wider social, moral and political questions about its purpose.

My aim in this book, then, is to consider the development of university teaching in both the detail of its practice and in terms of the values of the academic and social communities in which we live. To return to my illustration of the books by Barnett and Entwistle, I want to engage with the sociological interests of the former as well as the psychological inclinations of the latter. But in doing so, I shall not attempt to review wide and fragmented literatures that have informed thinking about these matters.

Background to this enquiry

My approach will be to present a somewhat personal exploration, rather than a scholarly review. I shall draw heavily upon my own first-hand experience, and attempt to bring that experience to life, rather than reflect in detail upon the contributions of others. Significantly, perhaps, such an approach has also been adopted (Boud *et al.* 1993) by the one writer, David Boud, to whom both Entwistle and Barnett made reference in the work cited above.

One consequence of this being a personal enquiry is that I should start off by saying a little about myself – 'where I come from' – in order that the reader can start to orientate their own situation to mine. Some understanding of the differences and similarities between the writer's and reader's experience and perspective should help the reader to view this text critically, rather than as a handbook of good practice.

Perhaps as a consequence of the fragmentation referred to above, and a lack of a shared sense of the purpose of higher education, many university teachers have told me that they don't see themselves as 'real' or 'ordinary' academics. In a similar way, many department heads I have spoken to have claimed that their department is different from others in the institution. I also do not see myself as an ordinary academic.

After a brief career in the military, which I left as a conscientious objector, and a period of studying engineering and then philosophy, I taught primary school children. Fascinated by the intelligence of the young child, before the system of formal education has had too strong a stranglehold, I wrote about children's classroom learning (Rowland 1984) and encouraged other teachers to do the same. My present view about understanding learning, which I shall pursue in this book, has its roots in that experience. In particular, it values an important principle about investigating learning.

This is that the people who are best placed to understand the processes of learning are those who teach. This is not to say that all university teachers (or primary school teachers) are experts, or even well informed, about the nature of student learning. It is that the role of the teacher provides the best possible vantage point from which to understand learning. An important consequence of this was the conclusion I drew that the best forms of teaching are those in which the teacher is also finding out about the learner. Now it might seem that such a view immediately casts doubt on the value of the mass lecture as a method of teaching. For how can a lecturer find much out about the learning of, say, 200 students? Teaching, however, consists of more than just lecturing: assessing students' work; designing curricula; gaining student feedback on teaching; tutorial work; learning which is mediated by new information technologies; and so on. Taken as a whole, lectures have their place. What I am suggesting here is simply that, in relation to the whole range of teaching activities, for teachers to be effective they need to be finding out what and how their students are learning.

To put it candidly, if, as teachers, we are not gaining insight into the nature of our students' learning, then we are not teaching properly. The teacher's enquiry into their students' learning is not only a valuable form of educational enquiry, it is also the most valuable approach to teaching. In other words, enquiring into our teaching is not only an activity that produces useful 'findings' about our teaching, but it is also one that directly improves the quality of teaching in the very process of conducting the enquiry.

It follows from this that we should view with some scepticism the findings of those who claim that they are experts about the practice of other people. This, of course, applies to this book. It does not offer expertise about the reader's or anyone else's practice (except, perhaps, my own).

Following my move into higher education, I initially taught on professional development courses for school teachers. My study of that (Rowland 1993) clarified for me another theme that is also important in this book; the realization that the judgements that we make as teachers are often in response to *dilemmas*. A dilemma is a situation in which two principles are in conflict with each other. Unlike problems, which, in principle, have solutions (even if we are unable to grasp them), dilemmas do not have solutions. They are choices we have to make in the face of conflicting principles.

For example, Chris's decision to hold a tutorial for his students that he would not attend presented him with a dilemma. By being present he would have been acting upon his principle that he should support his students' learning. By being absent he would be acting upon his principle that students should be responsible for their own learning. The choice he made was a judgement in the face of this dilemma.

Thus, teaching is not a matter of following a set of rules, or theories, or steps, but more a matter of making judgements in the face of conflicting priorities, which are different in different situations. These priorities or principles often express our values. Reflecting upon these dilemmas can bring us closer to understanding our values and developing our teaching so that it expresses them more fully.

Such an emphasis reinforces the need to view with some scepticism the pronouncements of experts about the best methods of teaching. It also serves to remind us that the choices we make are a question not only of teaching technique, but also of values.

Over the past seven years I have worked almost exclusively with teachers in the higher education sector. The programme in which Chris took part was a Masters course in teaching and learning for university lecturers that has been running since 1992. As well as designing and teaching this course, I have been involved in a number of collaborative activities with colleagues in the UK and other countries that have aimed at developing teaching and exploring the values that underlie it. Working in such widely different social contexts has again made me aware of the extent to which the ways we teach are related to larger questions about the purposes of higher education and the society it serves.

The material for this book is drawn from this range of activity. It includes reports of small scale research, writings of a reflective kind that arise from my attempts to understand my own problems and illustrative anecdotes from the experiences of other university teachers. My approach to writing, which I see as a fundamental part of the process of reflecting upon and theorizing professional practice, adopts a variety of forms, including fictional writing.

I chose to work in a university because I enjoy, like many of my colleagues, intellectual community. Like many others, I also feel that the space left for reflection is threatened by our increasingly pressurized working life. It is clear to me that the most important feature of any environment that promotes our professional development, and thus the learning of our students, is one that includes such reflective space. I hope to show how such space might be created and used.

A map to guide your journey through this book

Any discussion of the development of university teaching immediately raises the question of what priority this should be given in relation to research.

The assumption behind such questions is that teaching and research impose competing pressures on the working life of the academic, and in most universities in the so-called developed world, academics are rewarded for their research efforts over and above their teaching. These observations prompt us to ask what is, and what should be, the relationship between teaching and research. This raises further questions about whether or not one's teaching is supported by one being actively involved in research. At a time when the UK and other countries are giving more serious attention to improving the quality of university teaching, more light needs to be shed on these questions.

The relationships between teaching and research, and how these are understood by academics in my own institution, are the subject of Chapter 2. A study of this question indicates a set of principles or values upon which might be constructed programmes for the development of teaching and learning. The aim here is to design a strategy for academics to develop their teaching in ways that are fitting for a university culture that values research in the disciplines.

Chapter 3 gives an account of how we constructed a course based upon these principles at my own institution. There is a general recognition, in the UK at least, that strategies to develop university teaching should be developed within the institutions themselves (Institute of Learning and Teaching Planning Group (ILTPG) 1998: 14). This is because such strategies should reflect the different purposes and priorities of different institutions, and relate to their own particular contexts. I make no attempt to review the range of such provisions that have emerged in different institutions and contexts, but instead consider, in more detail, how we have designed a programme appropriate to our own priorities. It is significant, however, that this programme – the course in which Chris who introduced this chapter played a part – was among the first Masters level courses in teaching and learning for university staff. It is also significant that this development took place in an institution that sees itself as being 'research led'. At the end of 1998, we surveyed all those who had taken part over seven years since the course started. In Chapter 3 I will refer to this survey in order to assess the ways in which the aims of the programme were reflected in changes in the participants' working practices, including their research output as well as their teaching. Since the course participants are university teachers, it is important to consider how the course process may provide a model for their work with undergraduate students.

It will become clear how this course values open negotiation, a sensitivity to group processes and a facilitative role for the course tutor. Such terms as 'student centred', 'facilitation' and 'negotiation' are now widely used, particularly in discussions about adult learning. Wide use, however, does not necessarily indicate clarity, and such terms, as they become part of an educational jargon, are in danger of losing their meaning. Their use often indicates little more than a rejection of customary practices rather than a clear articulation of how to work with students. If we are to give some clarity to such notions, we need to be more specific about the kind of learning that is taking place, how it takes place and how it may be promoted. This suggests some kind of 'pedagogy' for the learning of the academic.

Pedagogical theory is the subject of Chapter 4. Drawing upon the experiences and interpretations offered in Chapters 2 and 3, I reflect here on the nature of theory in the context of this kind of developmental work. Why do we need educational theory? What is an educational theory? Such questions are not at all straightforward and the chapter ends on a note of uncertainty. I do, however, derive a 'model' (which may be thought of as a kind of theory), which underlies my claim that there are interesting links between teaching and the ways of thinking that are involved in academic research in disciplines other than education. The model sheds some light on the kind of professional development described in Chapter 3, and highlights the value that can be gained by lecturers working in mixed groups across the disciplines. It thus also addresses my central concern in this book to speak across the divides between higher education teachers.

The term 'critical' is often used to describe the educational objectives of university teaching; we want our students to think 'critically'. The model I outline here indicates how a critical approach to learning is also important for the learning (about teaching) of university teachers. Unless our own professional development encourages us to take a critical approach to our studies, how can we expect our students to adopt such an approach to their learning?

It is one thing to hope that our students will approach their studies critically; quite another for us to be placed in the role of student in which we are expected to be critical. This is the position in which lecturers find themselves as students on a course designed for their professional development. This change in roles – from teacher to learner – can be both disturbing and illuminating for the lecturer, particularly when its subject matter is their own teaching. It also raises problems for the tutor on any such course, who is now in the role of a teacher of colleagues whose academic experience, and possibly status, may be in advance of their own (however that might be judged).

In Chapter 5 I shall consider this experience in more detail and in relation to the model introduced in Chapter 4. Drawing upon my own journal notes, the comments of course participants, transcripts of course meetings and electronically mediated discussion, I will lead us to consider a number of dilemmas. Some of these concern the relationships of power and control between student and teacher. I am not referring here to the problem for lecturers in maintaining control over unruly or disenchanted students, although this can be real enough in some contexts. The issue here arises from the fact that I (like Chris in the above example about a tutorless tutorial) believe in two principles that seem to pull in opposite directions: the first is that learners are ultimately responsible for their own learning; the second is that teachers, within the constraints afforded by their context, are responsible for their teaching. The old adage 'you can take a horse to water but you can't make it drink' nicely describes this situation. However, if the effectiveness of our teaching is to be judged by the effectiveness of our students' learning, then we are to be judged not only in terms of whether we succeed in 'taking our horses to water', but whether we can 'ensure that they drink'. In this angst-ridden situation our teaching is judged in terms of something (student learning) that is not our responsibility. It is hardly surprising, then, that questions of power and control arise as we, and our students, grapple with the uncertainties over who is *really* responsible for students' learning.

Such questions are addressed in relation to the details of actual inter-actions between lecturers (as they enquire into their teaching) and their tutors. These explorations help us to understand our educational values and how these can be implemented in better teaching. But conversation is ephem-eral. It leaves little trace of our thinking and little opportunity to explore it in greater depth. Helpful though it is to talk through our problems, the situation we find ourselves in as teachers sometimes requires a more reflect-ive approach in order to discover what we really think and feel. Writing can provide the space for this deeper kind of enquiry.

In academic life generally, writing is the normal means by which invest-igation is reported. Few academic journals, however, give explicit attention to the process of writing, and academic writing is rarely seen as being an important *process* of investigation. There has recently been a growing inter-est in the ways in which the process of reflective, imaginative and even fictional writing can help us to gain a better understanding of the prob-lems, values and feelings related to our personal and professional lives (see, for example, Bolton 1999, Winter *et al.* 1999).

Talk about 'feelings' in relation to teaching may seem far removed from the concern to develop effective techniques, or build 'competence'. Many teachers, however, speak of their 'passion' for teaching or their 'love' of their subject, their 'frustration' about the context in which they find themselves or their 'anger' in response to the pressures under which they work. The impact that such emotional responses have upon our teaching is profound. The intellectual life of the academic is not just a dry, problem-solving exer-cise, and teaching, in particular, is an altogether human activity.

A colleague, Peter, who was part of the same group as Chris, completed a lengthy study of his own teaching and development of a new course for students of dentistry. A conclusion to his study was the enormous import-ance he attached to what he called 'a love of the subject'. He felt, however, that it was difficult to write about this; difficult to see how the development of his teaching might more adequately reflect his own love for his subject and thereby stimulate the same feeling in his students. In Chapter 6 I consider how writing about our teaching might address this kind of feeling in order to give it a more prominent role in our teaching. Such kinds of writing and enquiry might seem unusual to a teacher who, like Peter, is more familiar with academic investigation, which values objectivity, proof and certainty rather than the shifting sands of personal feelings. In Chapter 6

I indicate how the kind of enquiry that takes full account of the emotional dimensions of our work as teachers might involve forms of writing that are unfamiliar in the academic work of most university teachers.

But a discussion of these matters needs a practical example. Exactly what can be learnt from writing about these things and how can it influence our practice? Chapter 7 provides an example. It takes the form of two sequential texts. One is a fictional story based closely upon the experience of providing consultative support for a project on teaching and learning in the newly democratic South Africa. The second text, written a year or so later, reflects upon the story, interprets it and identifies what I learnt from writing it.

From this introduction, it has already become clear that the development of our teaching involves the kind of personal enquiry and openness to change that inform our ability to make educational judgements in the light of personal and professional values. Without this, skills alone will not equip us to respond to the changing and often unpredictable circumstances of teaching. Such a form of learning, however, might appear to verge upon therapy. In Chapter 8 I touch upon the similarities and distinctions between learning and therapy, drawing upon the comments of academics, and relating closely to the model developed in Chapter 4.

The values that underlie our teaching are influenced by the social and political circumstances in which we teach. These vary across the different higher education institutions in the UK. Cultural differences, however, become even more marked when we work with colleagues and students from different countries. As higher education is increasingly seen as moving into the 'global economy', we need to think about how the values underlying our own teaching may, or may not, conform to those of our overseas colleagues and students. New technologies may facilitate almost instant communication between people in different cultures, but it does not thereby eradicate cultural difference.

Drawing upon work with university teachers from different countries, including Russia and South Africa (which is significant because both countries are undergoing radical social changes), in the second part of the chapter I consider to what extent teaching methods are a reflection of political and social values.

In Chapters 1–8 I have told the story of my own enquiry. In Chapter 9 I shift the focus and give more explicit attention to the kind of questions which you, the reader, might have as you attempt to embark upon your own journey of enquiry. My responses will lead towards a conception of academic work in which teaching can be a critical and intellectually rewarding activity that draws academics together for the development of themselves and each other as teachers and researchers.

2

The Relationship Between Teaching and Research

The changing role of the university teacher

Can university teachers really afford to devote much time to a serious enquiry into their teaching given the pressures of disciplinary research? Or, to put this another way, can teachers who are *interested* in their research also be expected to show the same interest in their teaching?

The *Oxford English Dictionary* defines a *university* as: 'The whole body of teachers and students pursuing, at a particular pace, the higher branches of learning'. Even this brief definition suggests a link between teaching and research. They are both about learning: our learning and our students' learning. In order to address these questions, then, we need to clarify the nature of the relationship between our pursuit and our students' pursuit of learning.

Several studies have sought to address the question of whether good university teachers are also good researchers. Much of this work has been inconclusive (Terenzini and Pascarella 1994), although recent research suggests some of the ways in which students value their teachers' involvement in research (Jenkins *et al.* 1998). My purpose here, however, is not to find out whether good teachers are also good researchers. Such an investigation has little point unless we are clear about what we mean by 'good teaching' and 'good research'. For our purposes, it is more important to explore how our teaching, our learning, our students' learning and our research might be brought into more productive relationships. This is what I shall explore in this chapter in order to provide a framework for how university teachers might develop the quality of student learning through some form of sustained enquiry.

But first let us place this discussion in context. In the early 1960s, when the proportion of young people going on to higher education in the UK was around 6 per cent (Committee on Higher Education 1963: 46), it was possible for the university lecturer, with some confidence, to conceive that their scholarly role was 'not as an employee but as a free citizen of the academic community' (Gustad 1966: 12). It is envisaged that by 2002, in addition to a rising number of mature university students, the proportion of young people who will participate in higher education in the UK will be 35 per cent (DfEE 1998b: 15). Is it fanciful to imagine that university teachers will still be able to conceive of themselves in such a scholarly role, pursuing their interests as 'free citizens' while providing the workforce to educate (or is it train) this increased student body?

The role of the university teacher is changing; the idea of what counts as a university lacks clear criteria; and in the UK even the demand to expand is uncertain and has changed with abrupt swings of government policy (Sutherland 1994). The confidence of the 1960s is a distant memory. In this changing climate there is a generally acknowledged need to re-examine the relationship between teaching and research and the parts they play in the work of university teachers who are seriously concerned to develop their teaching. This is not just a matter of establishing the relative importance of each, but of exploring 'the more essential issue: what does it mean to be a scholar' (Boyer 1994: 116).

It is, however, in terms of our teaching and research that our productivity as academics, and that of our institutions, is measured by those who provide the funds. These are the terms in which we feel the pressures of accountability through recent initiatives, in the UK and elsewhere, to assess the quality of research and teaching.

To help with this exploration, I have drawn upon the perspectives of a dozen 'informants': experienced academics in my own institution, a large 'old' university in the North of England. It is important to emphasize here that the views I was gathering were those of influential academics in my own institution, which sees itself as being 'research led'. The situation might be viewed differently in the newer universities that have traditionally seen themselves as stronger in teaching than research. Given the rapidly changing nature of higher education, it is important not to be too ready to generalize across institutions. My purpose here was to restrict the enquiry to my own institution, since that was context for my own professional development activity. At other institutions, similar investigation might reveal a different culture, which should be reflected in different programmes.

I selected my interviewees to represent a cross-section of university departments: arts and sciences; vocational and non-vocational subjects; pure and applied orientations; and large and small departments. Since I was interested in obtaining something of an overview from academics with considerable experience, each is the head of his department. I say 'his' here because, in fact, each was male. In a university of about 80 departments, only one head of department was female at the time of the study. No doubt this reflects the lack of equality of opportunity for women in academic life. I do not give adequate attention to this important issue here, although the effect of this imbalance will be seen to be significant.

I held informal tape-recorded interviews with each head of department concerning their views about teaching and research. I wanted to draw upon their wider professional experience, rather than enquire into specific departmental practices, in order to shed some light on the debate about teaching and research. My hope was that such an enquiry in my own institution would provide valuable insight into the university's culture. Any programmes to develop teaching would need to be informed by the values and expectations of those who work in it. The development of university teaching is, particularly at present, a politically charged subject. I envisaged that this study would help me to position developing programmes in relation to the politicized and shifting priorities between teaching and research.

From these interviews a line of argument develops based on the experience of academics. It is not a case study of the informants, or of their departments; it makes no claim to represent a complete picture of the particular university or, even less, of academic workers in general. It does, however, indicate some far-reaching principles for how the problem of improving learning might be tackled.

Priorities in teaching and research

When asked about the relative importance of teaching and research all my respondents thought that teaching and research should co-exist in a balance within any department. They all felt that *in principle* every university teacher should be involved in both aspects of the work, that they were both equally important, and they were reluctant to give one priority over the other. In this respect, it seems, things have not changed since Halsey and Trow (1971) conducted their detailed survey on the British academic at the end of the 1960s.

This dominant perspective reflects what some have called the 'liberal' view of the university. Scott (1984: 64) contrasts this view with that of the 'modern' university, in which the 'professionalization of academic knowledge has made it increasingly difficult to regard teaching and research as harmonious activities'. Even in 1984 he was suggesting that such 'liberal' sentiments as British academics express are 'a measure of the anachronism of the system'. Scott's view is not shared, however, across the higher education sector. In 1999, the Vice-chancellor of Cambridge University saw the need to emphasize these 'liberal' sentiments, by claiming that 'it is entirely artificial to separate teaching and research' (Broers 1999).

In opposition to this ideology, many British universities have more recently been likened to universities in the USA, where, it has been suggested, such a 'deep ideological commitment' to liberal values may have been largely replaced by a 'need to survive' (Phillips 1994: 54), in which liberal values have no place. While my respondents in general appeared to express a personal commitment to the liberal idea that teaching and research should be integral, many recognized that this was made difficult by the pressures of accountability in terms of research output. Keeping the two together was, for them, no easily gained 'harmonious activity'.

While some entered their academic career with a major interest in teaching, and others with their initial interest in research, they all saw research as being the more influential in leading to promotion. In discussions about the qualities of the researcher (as contrasted with the teacher), one talked of the need for more 'single-mindedness' in research than in teaching. Another expressed this idea at more length: 'A researcher should be – I don't know whether selfish is quite the right word – but somebody who has a passion for something and wants to pursue it at all costs . . . I wouldn't apply that to a teacher quite in that way because I think you have to be much more open as a teacher'.

Others used terms such as 'drive', 'self-motivation', 'stickability', 'confidence' and the ability to 'go out into the world and get it'. Put together, these male respondents have described the personal qualities of the successful researcher in terms that closely conform to male stereotypes, whereas successful teaching required 'openness', 'concern for students' and 'caring', and was often carried out with a sense of duty. Such qualities are more often associated with female stereotypes. It cannot be altogether coincidental that these representatives of a largely male preserve of senior academics reflect a view of research (which has been the main criterion for their gaining seniority) in terms of primarily male qualities. There would seem to be no obvious epistemological basis for this view of knowledge and its production. Such a perspective is no doubt self-reinforcing of the male hierarchy that produces it.

It may be that in universities, as in industrial organizations, male employees have resisted the advancement of women (Cockburn 1989), and that this accounts for why research – which is the key to promotion – is understood in such male terms. From my senior, male respondents, there seemed to be no awareness that their views about the qualities of the researcher might favour males; indeed the suggestion was strongly rejected by some when the findings were reported. It may be, however, that at a deeper and unconscious level this kind of gender stereotyping has influenced the very way we think about research and teaching.

Several also saw research, rather than teaching, as the academic's 'own work'. This view also confirms that of Halsey and Trow (1971) and more recent reports (Elton and Partington 1993: 4). The predominance of such a view sets up a tension about the way people see their working life and compare themselves with their colleagues. This is how one head of department expressed the problem:

> One of the striking things about people who basically only are good at teaching is they don't see research as work. They can't write themselves, but they are very envious people. For example, if people say . . . they want to be away (to do research), these people think they are not working, doing research is not working, reading is not working.

Furthermore, there was general agreement, especially in the less vocationally oriented departments, that research (rather than teaching) was the prime factor in departmental, as well as individual, advancement. Several mentioned that there were dangers in spending too much time on teaching. No one suggested that they needed to warn people against spending too much time on research.

Nearly all the heads of department I interviewed thought that *in principle* teaching and research were equally important, and indeed a few, whose departments were more involved in professional training, considered teaching to be a more important part of their role. Why then did they view research as being more highly valued *in practice*?

Why does teaching have a lower status?

Part of the answer to this is financial. The recent arrangements for funding teaching and research in British universities were generally held to favour research measures rather than teaching measures as being the more significant determinant of future funding, but there were differences of view and some uncertainty about how this would work and how it would feed into the quality of learning.

Most regretted such an undue bias towards research at the expense of teaching, but not all. One respondent explained how an emphasis upon improving the research rating (and thus the funding that is attached to this) is the most effective way of improving the quality of teaching, because it would draw in extra funds, which could be used to reduce class size and thus improve learning. Another thought that an improvement in research rating would enhance the department's reputation and make it more attractive to students, thereby enabling the department to select a higher quality student intake, which, he felt, would improve the quality of learning. While there was a variety of expectations about how funding arrangements might influence the quality of learning and in what direction, there was no doubt that research measures, rather than teaching measures, would be more significant.

Without any prompting, almost every respondent said that one reason why teaching was valued less than research was because of the difficulties of assessing teaching. Research, it was argued, could be assessed by the traditional methods of peer review leading to publication (although several had criticisms of how this worked in practice). Teaching, on the other hand, is a largely private affair. Many offered the kind of view eloquently expressed by Halsey and Trow: 'One of the chief disadvantages of being primarily a teacher is that one's reputation, however well earned, is essentially intangible, and wide recognition depends on the word-of-mouth communication of one's colleagues' (1971: 336); or put more colourfully by Becher and Kogan: 'Like sex among the British, teaching has remained in the realm of the private, the unspoken and the amateur' (1980: 106).

This amusing parallel is perhaps worth taking seriously. Foucault (1981) has argued that the development of a language of sexuality in Western culture over the past century or so has not had the liberating effect that some have imagined but has, on the contrary, led to greater opportunities for centralized control as behaviour has become more precisely categorized and open to legislation. In a similar fashion, might the emergence of a more public discourse of teaching and learning also lead to greater centralized control and conformity? As centralized bodies (such as the Institute for Learning and Teaching (ILT) in the UK) stimulate more debate, perhaps control and conformity will result, rather than exploration and innovation. How desirable would this be? This is an issue I shall return to in Chapter 6 in relation to writing about teaching.

Another way of looking at the difficulties of measuring teaching was put by one respondent like this:

> Given [that] the people who've got to the top are actually mostly good researchers in many cases – they may be quite good individual teachers – but they have never thought about teaching development as important . . . We have to have a whole range of criteria (for judging teaching) and then people have to be educated as to what those criteria are.

So the problem may not be, perhaps, as many of the respondents thought, that teaching is essentially any more difficult to assess than research. It may merely be that those in positions of power have given little thought as to how to do this. This is an in-built conservatism of the university system: only those whose work is valued gain status, and in turn confer status on those whose work expresses the same qualities.

The problem then becomes how the evaluation of teaching is to be institutionalized. From his experience of higher education in the USA, Boyer (1994: 128) has spoken about how peer evaluation, student evaluation and self-evaluation have the potential for creating this kind of change. The recent moves to assess teaching on a national basis in the UK, however, were felt by some of my respondents to fall short of this mark, even though the intention of giving greater value to teaching was welcomed. One head of a department that had only recently been assessed and graded as 'Excellent' in teaching put it rather forcefully:

> The teaching assessment is an absolute monster which had nothing to do with the real world at all . . . it's about whether we have in place mechanisms that make sure that quality doesn't vary. So what! I'd rather take some risks I think. I'd rather have staff that make terrible mistakes but who also occasionally reach enormous heights, than have everybody worrying about paper work.

Any attempt to institutionalize the evaluation of teaching must be based upon an adequate understanding of the relationships between teaching and research. But first we need to understand how these categories are used.

The categories of teaching and research

A university is a complex organization of academic staff who come from widely ranging disciplinary cultures, or 'tribes' as Becher (1989) calls them. An academic in dentistry, for example, may have less in common with a historian in the same institution than with practitioners in the medical profession. Most of my respondents wanted to point out to me that their department was a special case in some way or other. They are nevertheless all held to account, in the university setting, in terms of their teaching and their research. But how useful are the concepts of 'teaching' and 'research' for describing their practice? Bourdieu (1988: 13) has argued that such typifications of the roles of academics 'prevent us from conceptualizing the university field' because they fail to recognize the particular case in all its complexity and how particular practices reflect the principles that under-pin them. This is a limitation of wide ranging surveys (such as Halsey and Trow 1971) and also of general discussions (such as Elton and Partington 1993), which, in other ways, have thrown light on the teaching versus research debate.

These difficulties were reflected in much that my respondents said about how they used the terms 'teaching' and 'research'. For example, in several cases, the term 'teaching' was understood by the respondents to mean 'giving lectures', whereas 'research supervision' was seen as an aspect of the academic's research (this especially in the sciences). On the other hand, a head of an interdisciplinary department considered that some of his staff viewed giving lectures as a means by which their research was disseminated, and was therefore part of the research role; whereas research supervision, because of its interactional and educational character, was seen as being part of the teaching role.

One way of resolving this category distinction is in terms of the audience for the activity. Thus, presenting one's research as a lecture to a group of students counts as teaching, whereas presenting the same lecture in the same manner to a group of academic peers counts as research. This distinc-tion reflects the separation between teaching and research in terms of funding and in terms of the status differential between those learners who are students and those who are researchers. A problem with using this criterion of audience (student or peer) to distinguish between the research and teaching roles is that it disallows the possibility that one might conduct one's research with the collaboration of students. The general accept-ance of this criterion is, however, indicated by the fact that few would describe the dissemination of their research to their peers as being part of an academic's teaching role. One respondent was clear, however, that a seminar for peers was indeed an instance of teaching. Even the publica-tion of a learned paper, he argued, was an attempt to communicate ideas and thus foster learning, or teach. For him, the dissemination of research is a pedagogical activity and therefore to separate teaching and research is illogical.

A more cynical distinction was the suggestion that when academic staff learn, it is the result of research, but when students learn it is the result of teaching. But most of those interviewed saw learning as being much more a two-way process. Here, a head of an engineering department describes a difficulty with trying to separate teaching and research in the way that is demanded by the assessment initiatives: 'In undergraduate teaching we have final year projects. Quite a lot of them are done in collaboration with industry. Now is that teaching? Is it research? It is certainly education. Some of those projects can have an immediate impact on . . . [the lecturer's] own research.'

Several respondents said that when they taught students by means of a lecture they 'talked down to them' in a way that they did not have to with their peers. In this way a teaching lecture was different from a research lecture. In preparing to 'talk down to them' the lecturer had to devise simple and coherent structures by which a complex subject matter could be communicated and put into context. One described how this requirement to structure and relate the work to fundamental ideas in the field sometimes gave an added or changed meaning to his own research. This teaching preparation then became part of his research process.

What became clear was that although people normally used the terms teaching and research in a relatively unproblematic fashion, once some of them began to think of their academic activity in more specific detail, the two terms became much more closely intertwined. In some cases, respondents were reluctant even to make distinctions between them except in the most superficial of contexts. In other words, the category distinction between teaching and research may owe more to the demands for accountability than to logical or pedagogical differences between academic roles.

This uncertainty about the distinctions, conceptually, between teaching and research has important implications for how we understand any serious enquiry into the development of our own teaching within our subject field. It suggests that such enquiry might be seen as being closely connected to research in the field and not just to *educational* research. Indeed, in the UK it is envisaged that future research assessment exercises will require the panels who judge the quality of research in their field *also* to state how they are going to assess research into the teaching of the field (Rogers 1999). But if there is this connection between research and teaching, what exactly is its nature?

The links between teaching and research

One head of department who had just been explaining to me how some of his colleagues saw their research as being teaching on a different level said: 'No one's ever asked me about teaching before. It's really quite interesting!' The implication of his remark in this context seemed to be that since research interested him, and he felt it was so closely related to teaching, then teaching must be interesting too.

All those interviewed expressed a view that active involvement in the research process directly improved the quality of teaching. The reasons given for this were: it casts the academic in the role of learner and therefore helps them understand the learning experience; it promotes a critical engagement with the subject matter; it keeps the academic up to date with the frontiers of knowledge within the discipline. Such linkages are to be expected.

Two related factors, however, emerged to be important determinants of just *how* closely the two are related: the first concerned the academic's approach to the field of research; the second concerned their approach to teaching.

In different ways, many heads of department considered that what might loosely be termed a 'broad' approach to research was more closely related to teaching than one that was narrow or specialized. The term 'broad' seemed to apply to research aimed at developing a critique of matters of fundamental concern in the discipline (and therefore important for any student within the discipline); or research that was interdisciplinary (and thus related to students' broader interests); or research aimed at applying the discipline to a social or technical context (and thus relating to students' appreciation of a wider world outside the university). Many complained that the measures used to assess research strongly discouraged a broad approach, with its closer relationship to teaching, in favour of a narrow one. This is interesting in the light of the fact that, as far back as 1992, the Higher Education Funding Council of England (HEFCE) recognized that its method for assessing university research (the research assessment exercise) was perceived to have a negative effect on teaching (HEFCE 1992: 11).

The scope of this study was not sufficient to develop a precise analysis of the notion of breadth, nor its possible correlation with the disciplinary basis of the departments. The interviews, however, appeared to confirm the argument developed by Becher and Kogan (1980) that the relationship between the breadth of academic pursuit and its disciplinary basis is not fixed. For example, while it was suggested that pure science departments will more naturally practise narrow approaches to research, this popular stereotype was also contradicted by a scientist whom I interviewed.

Some instances of such a broad approach might shed some light on ways in which research might bear on teaching. A head of a medical department described how the insights gained from his research in community care, with its concern for the social context, was often applied to his teaching. A mathematician explained how the aesthetic experience of research at the frontiers of mathematics, and its concern to simplify mathematical structures – a fundamental issue in mathematics – had a direct bearing on helping first year undergraduates appreciate the subject. A literary critic claimed that insights from critical studies related to one author – the subject of his own research – could often be applied in teaching undergraduates studying different authors.

Such linkages were in addition to the more obvious instances of academics teaching their own particular research specialism. It was a policy in some departments that staff should teach in the area of their research wherever possible, but in other cases it was thought that this would lead to an undue bias in the undergraduate curriculum towards the particular interests of staff.

The second determinant that appeared to link teaching and research related to the approach to teaching. The key feature here was the extent of student–teacher interaction. In more interactional settings, such as projects, tutorials and seminars, the relationship between teaching and research was held to be much closer. This was not only because it provided an opportunity for the lecturer to teach their own speciality, but because the students' contributions offered new perspectives on the lecturer's own field of research, at times even challenging its assumptions. Instances were also provided of student projects leading academics to develop a new research idea within their existing field, or alternatively of stimulating them to move into different fields of investigation. But against this opportunity for a more collaborative approach to learning, several spoke of a culture of university lecturing in which students do not expect to ask questions or offer their own opinions.

Teaching that really encourages students to raise their own questions and offer alternative perspectives is, however, much less secure and predictable than more traditional lecturing methods, as several of the respondents pointed out. It demands that the lecturer present their knowledge as being open to question and related to the wider experience of the students. It encourages a range of questions from the students that cannot always be predicted in advance.

For this reason, it was suggested that only the more experienced and confident are able to teach in such a way that students are encouraged to challenge and question the lecturer's ideas. For example, one interviewee described how his own process of development in teaching and research over some years had led him to realize 'that all knowledge is situated and has an interest'. He continued: 'I'm always saying to students that nothing is right because somebody says it is right, and that includes me . . . That's almost a self-deconstructing statement'.

It is also an approach to teaching that encourages students to be critical, which is an aim of many higher education courses and, arguably, an aim of higher education itself. Where the lecturer can enable the students to 'deconstruct' the lecture, there is a direct pay-off for the research. For while it imbues teaching with the same critical orientation as research, it keeps the subject matter of the research alive and open to further enquiry.

The importance of students' learning being a 'critical' engagement for both teacher and learner was a notion that was expressed by many of the interviewees. It also confirmed the view that although some academics are better at teaching, and others more suited to research, the best teachers were often considered to be the most accomplished researchers. For them the commitment to the view that their research was always open to further critique or investigation could not to be set aside just because they were working with undergraduates.

Lecturers who have the skills to facilitate their students' questioning and can handle the uncertainties of group dynamics are at an advantage. But this is not just a question of teaching technique. What seemed to be important in these discussions was how this relationship between teaching and research depended upon how knowledge is conceived. Where knowledge is seen as being absolute, specialized and unrelated to wider perspectives or experiences of life, working with less knowledgeable students is unlikely to stimulate research. But where the knowledge that research produces is seen, *and is offered to students,* as being tentative, open to reinterpretation or containing insights that can be applied more widely, the ways that students relate to this knowledge are potentially significant to the lecturer's own research.

In other words, the approach to teaching that is linked most closely to research is one in which significance is given to what the students have to say, and opportunity is provided for their voices to be heard. Several heads of department who saw their own research as having been at the heart of their academic life attached this kind of significance to interaction with students.

To summarize, two hypotheses are suggested by what these interviewees had to say. First, an approach to teaching that emphasizes its interactive nature and applies to it the critical orientation of research, can enhance the research by which it is informed. And second, such an approach to teaching is held to be the most effective. If both are true, it follows that the most effective teaching is supportive of research. Narrow measures used to assess research and uninformed approaches to assessing teaching refuse to acknowledge either of these claims.

This perspective assumes that students have something of significance to contribute to the subject matter, albeit from a position of less experience. The realities of university teaching may sometimes seem far from this ideal, but we might take heart from the apocryphal comment of the philosopher Wittgenstein, who, while teaching at a university and reflecting on the time he had spent teaching at a kindergarten school, said that a classroom of young children was, for him, the most stimulating intellectual environment.

Research directly related to teaching and learning

The closest linkage between teaching and research arose when interviewees were asked how they viewed research that was directly concerned with teaching. There were extreme differences of view as to whether such investigation counted as research or not. In a humanities subject a head of department said that such research was not something to which he felt members of his department could usefully contribute. It was something for educationalists: 'No I don't think we would regard ourselves as qualified to do so. I could certainly give some ideas as to what I thought teaching was about . . . but if I were to write about teaching I would really feel that I ought to have studied teaching and know a bit more about teaching than I do'. In contrast, however, an architect said: 'If you look down the list of current research projects (in our department), probably nine out of ten of them are directly to do with teaching'. A head of department of medical general practice described how, from early in his academic career, he had been involved in research into teaching and this had been a chief interest ever since.

According to one argument, departments that have a stronger vocational orientation tend to be more involved with research into teaching. This is explained by the fact they are accountable to professional bodies for the quality of their graduates. This places pressure upon them to emphasize teaching (and thus consider research into teaching) even in an overall university environment that gives greater value to research.

A concern for research into teaching, however, was not evident only in vocationally oriented departments. For example, a head of a pure science department cited with some pride instances of research into teaching, some involving collaboration with other departments, that he had encouraged.

A head of an engineering department said that he valued research into teaching, but suggested that academics are discouraged by the promotion system from getting involved:

> It is very difficult to see how you can be a good teacher without being involved in that broader concept of research: you know, developing new case study material. OK it is all known, but you have to put it together, you have to make enquiries, you have to do research by going to the library, reading papers, talking to people. Now I think I would be quite happy to accept that as a research activity . . . but it wouldn't be very good on your CV for promotion.

It is interesting to place this comment beside the view of Professor Stewart Sutherland (then Vice-chancellor of London University):

> I would want to persuade colleagues that, for example, a chair in engineering education would be highly desirable. I am not sure we are getting engineering education right. We should give status to individuals who can think what engineering education is; what kinds of courses we provide, how we provide them, and how we can deliver them; and what form of engineering education is needed for the future.
>
> (Sutherland 1994: 15)

In the context of the preceding discussion, we should understand this statement as not just being about the importance of developing teaching skills, significant though this is. It requires *interdisciplinary* understanding to place academic fields, such as engineering, within their social and intellectual contexts. The development of interdisiplinary understanding in relation to teaching is an issue I shall consider in more detail in Chapter 4. As far as the present argument is concerned, the point is that this is not a case for giving teaching precedence *over* research, but suggests a strategy for ensuring that university education involves teaching that is aware of the wider context and the ways in which 'knowledge and understanding in these fields are always to some extent provisional' (Sutherland 1994: 10).

Implications for developing teaching through enquiry

In this section I draw together some of the strands of argument developed through these interviews with heads of department and suggest how they might indicate a strategy for an approach to the professional development of academic staff based upon sustained enquiry into our practice as university teachers.

The predominant perspective to emerge is one in which academics wished to be identified with a liberal tradition in which teaching and research were closely related aspects of their work, encouraging a critical and independent relation to knowledge. In spite of the fact that this perspective was seen to be under threat from demands for individual and departmental accountability, those interviewed were able to articulate in considerable detail the nature of this close relationship between teaching and research. It was not merely a cultural norm uncritically held, or an 'anachronism' from a lost past, as Scott maintained (1984: 64) but a view which grew, in most cases, out of the experience of doing teaching and research in what some called 'an environment of scholarship'.

The roots of this liberal tradition can be traced back through Cardinal Newman, in the nineteenth century (Newman 1976), to the writings of Plato two thousand years earlier (Plato 1971). We would want to resist some of the more élitist connotations associated with such traditional perspectives, reflecting as they do the undemocratic societies in which they emerged. The notion of 'scholarship', which was implicit in many of the discussions reported here, however, provides a basis for forms of academic development that seek to re-integrate teaching and research as part of a more democratic context. What would be the key features of such a programme for academic staff aimed at developing the quality of learning?

First, we need to develop an idea of critical interdisciplinarity (Barnett 1990). This could emerge if contexts were developed where lecturers could meet to draw upon the insights that their different disciplines offer to questions of teaching and learning. It is not a question of reducing teaching to a mechanical skill devoid of any disciplinary rigour. Nor is it simply a matter of identifying generic features of teaching and learning, for this would serve to exacerbate the tendency to separate teaching from research. Such contact will also enrich research by challenging assumptions that can become entrenched within particular disciplines. It can also serve to break down unhelpful stereotypes and academic tribalism (Becher 1989).

Second, such a programme must help academics to see the significance of students' perceptions of the subject matter and their learning. This will give a higher value to the students' contribution, thereby enhancing their learning and keeping the subject matter open to continual critique. This will mean developing strategies for encouraging students to express their ideas as part of the teaching process. It will also have considerable implications for how students are to be assessed.

Third, academics must be supported in developing ways of teaching that will inevitably feel risky and unpredictable as students become increasingly involved. This will also mean reconsidering such curriculum notions as 'learning outcomes' and 'objectives' in ways that acknowledge the unpredictable aspects of learning and include elements of a negotiated relationship between students and teachers.

Fourth, discussions among lecturers should seek to understand the relationships between the curriculum (and the research that informs it) and the context of students' lives and the wider society. This is a matter not of simply responding to commonplace assumptions about social needs, but of critically exploring the ways in which disciplinary knowledge is shaped by social forces while playing a part in shaping society. This will stimulate understanding of the connectedness of research, further help to break down artificial disciplinary boundaries and foster the transferability of students' knowledge to their lives beyond university.

Finally, lecturers should be encouraged to develop strategies for researching their own and each other's teaching processes. This will bring teaching, and its evaluation, into a public domain that is informed by a shared commitment to teaching rather than by bureaucratic demands for accountability. It will also begin to establish a field of practitioner research into higher education that draws upon the rich disciplinary knowledge across the university.

A programme of professional development with these aims might have many forms. It would involve meetings between staff. These would be more like a research forum than an instructional course on teaching methods. They would reflect the interdisciplinary, negotiative and socially aware aims of the programme. Discussion would be premised on a view of students as having something significant to say, and a view of lecturing staff that builds upon their research orientation. In meeting the needs of students for an improved environment for learning, it would also enliven research within and across disciplinary boundaries.

Conclusion

In this chapter I have drawn from an enquiry into the culture of my own institution with regard to teaching and research. This has confirmed some of the principles that I outlined in Chapter 1. These relate to the importance of engaging across disciplinary divides; the significance of what learners have to say; the inevitably unpredictable nature of learning; the importance of considering how the wider social context impacts upon our teaching; and the importance of sustained reflection upon teaching.

In Chapter 3 I want to show how a programme based on these principles has been developed in the same institution. This will bring us a little closer to the experience of learning about teaching.

3

Learning about Learning

Introduction

In 1992 Sheffield University initiated a Masters programme in teaching and learning for staff of the university. The programme, designed and tutored by Len Barton and myself, was to embody the approach to developing the teaching of academic staff through a process of sustained enquiry along the lines suggested in Chapter 2. While the course itself was very innovative at the time, the approach it adopts – which has been described as the Educational Researcher Model (Gosling 1997: 212–14) – is gaining a wider recognition. Its perspective is encapsulated in the advice given, by the editors, to contributors of the international journal *Teaching in Higher Education*, launched in 1996:

> They should adopt a questioning of critical approach in general, and particularly in relation to concepts such as 'quality', 'standards', or 'academic freedom' which are part of a professional discourse whose terms are often unexamined in the debates on higher education.
>
> (Barton 1996: 6)

Here I want to describe how this course was set up and discuss its outcomes in terms of the developments and changes in the practice of those who have participated. To do this, I shall draw upon earlier work which outlined the planning for the course (Rowland and Barton 1994) and a survey of all past participants conducted after the course had been running for seven years (Rowland and Skelton 1998).

There are dangers, of course, in telling the story of something one has been involved in over a period of years. With hindsight it is tempting to give, or perhaps impossible to avoid giving a gloss on past events in a way that imposes an orderliness upon them and forgets the untidiness that is an inevitable part of any developmental learning process. Furthermore, in the period since 1991 when the course was designed, there have been changes, not only in the UK, in the significance that teaching has in public debates about university education. I shall therefore say a few words about the wider context that led to setting up the course.

At the time of planning the course, the Committee of Vice-chancellars and Principals (CVCP) Academic Audit Unit (1992), 'a powerful catalyst for change', was half-way through work on its First Annual Report to the Director, based on a sample of 13 universities. While representing an increasing concern for the quality of university teaching, the assessment and account-ability of teaching was to be tightened up in the face of a rising student population. During the rest of the decade we have seen the effects of this tightening up, with regular assessments of teaching quality and, in 1999, the setting up of an institute for learning and teaching in higher education, the ILT. However, any clear conception of what was meant by 'quality' in this context was, at that time, difficult to perceive.

This lack of definition was matched by another ill-defined notion – 'en-terprise education' – which had gained increasing currency through the operations of the government funded Enterprise in Higher Education (EHE) initiative. While some viewed this initiative as a natural product of 1980s Thatcherite values of the market place, others (such as Bridges 1992) saw it as a package more consistent with a social democratic or liberal philosophy. Amid such ambiguity, there was general recognition of its concern to pro-mote 'student centred', 'active' and 'independent' approaches to learning. These terms had their roots in the experience of earlier government funded Technical and Vocational Education Initiative (TVEI) projects, which sought to develop such approaches in UK schools.

In this context, with its mixed ideological overtones, Sheffield University Division of Education was approached by the university's Staff Training and Development Unit (STDU), and the Enterprise Unit (funded by EHE) with a view to developing a Masters level course in teaching and learning for lecturers in the university. The purpose of such a course, it was suggested, would be to develop more 'student centred' approaches to learning across the university.

It seemed clear to me that any course that aimed to promote 'student centred' approaches would itself need to be student centred. I was attracted by the idea of working in this way with a student group of academics from across the university. Apart from Len Barton and myself, however, I remem-ber the uncertainty of many in my department of education about getting involved in a course that would inevitably have a high profile across the university. It was only to become clear over the following eight years that this reluctance of academic staff from university education departments to address teaching across their own institution was to prove significant.

At that time, the UK government's hostility towards educational theory and theorists was already becoming apparent, although it had not approached the strident levels it reached by 1998 in, for example, the Tooley Report (Tooley and Darby 1998). Instead of theory, it was argued, more emphasis should be given to 'teaching skills' developed in the classroom with a return to the 'tried and tested methods from the past' (Department of Education and Science (DES) 1991). We can now see these sentiments amplified in policy documents of the late 1990s.

While the training of school teachers was moving in this direction, there was every reason to fear that developments in higher education teaching would also place the emphasis upon narrowly conceived skills and competencies rather than any more critical understanding. Was this proposal for a course for university lecturers, then, merely an attempt to add 'teaching skills' to the repertoire of academic competencies? This would be consistent with those who, like Leftwich, saw EHE as being concerned with providing 'practical life and work skills [rather] than new or improved ways of sharpening intellectual and creative skills, interpretative understandings or critical judgements' (Leftwich 1991: 281). Or did its innovative concern with developing an award bearing course, at Masters level, suggest a recognition of the importance of such critical abilities in the development of teaching?

It was already clear to me that a programme based upon sustained and open-ended enquiry into practice was not necessarily what the managers and funders were looking for. In this respect, the situation at the start of the new millennium is perhaps even more difficult. For by this time any such course in teaching and learning is open to scrutiny and accreditation by a central body (the ILT), which is steeped in a discourse of skills and competencies. But at that time, it was clear that the kind of programme that I believe to be appropriate for the culture of the university as suggested in Chapter 2, would not necessarily reflect some of the externally imposed agendas. We would have to articulate our case clearly.

A framework for a course

Early discussions centred around the competing claims for theory and practice. One suggestion was that the course might be viewed as an extended induction, or initial training, for new lecturers, directed at the development of the basic skills of teaching: a kind of teacher training course for higher education lecturers. According to this view, the course should emphasize practice rather than theory. However, it was suggested that since many of our 'students' would already have PhDs, they would be competent to handle a more theoretical approach. For this reason it should be at Masters 'level'.

Discussions about the 'level' of the proposed course were not very productive, with questions of status being muddled with educational and epistemological issues. Since this was to be, as far as we were aware, the first Masters course in teaching to be put on for its own staff by an institution such as ours, there was little precedent to draw upon. Furthermore, discussions about 'level' are often underpinned by assumptions about the role of theory, a question that I shall consider in more detail in Chapter 4 in the light of our experience of running the course for eight years. At the time of these initial discussions prior to planning the course we were concerned to avoid a false dualism between theory and practice.

At a time of increasing regulation in teacher training, it was important that the proposed course should be seen as a critical engagement with the role and practice of the teacher in a university context, rather than a basic 'nuts and bolts' training. We wanted (as tutors as well as participants on the course) to develop our teaching through a process of sustained research directed towards our own and each other's practice. The course would thus be an enquiry for the tutors as well as for the students. This would mean much more than merely learning new techniques or 'transferable skills', which, according to National Foundation for Educational Research (NFER) (1991), appeared to be the main aim of the EHE.

With this research perspective in mind, our suggestion was that the course would address practical and technical matters as these arose from the participants' investigations into their own practice rather than provide planned instruction in teaching techniques. Furthermore the course would aim to raise fundamental questions concerning pedagogy – the relationships between teacher, student and subject matter – within the particular social context, rather than merely focus on methods in isolation. This would provide the basis for developing practice.

Broadly speaking, this might be viewed as an 'action research' process in which individuals seek to improve their practice of teaching by subjecting it to scrutiny and development as part of what Carr and Kemmis (1986) have called an 'emancipatory' project. Such an approach views teaching as a moral activity in which questions of intellectual and professional development cannot be divorced from matters of social justice.

Conceived in this way, the course would be altogether fitting for a Masters Degree oriented towards professional practice, rather than a narrowly conceived initial training course. But the centrality that it gives to the practice of teaching appeared to make it acceptable to those who had come to us with the proposal. On this basis we were now prepared to consider an overall framework within which a 'curriculum' for the course might emerge.

We planned for a group of 12 participants working with Len Barton and me as tutors on the course. In order to maximize the opportunities for learning across as wide a spectrum as possible, participants were to be drawn from a range of academic disciplines and levels of experience. They would have their fees met by the university, but would be expected to fulfil all their normal teaching, research and administrative duties as well.

Although 12:2 would seem to be an 'uneconomic' student–tutor ratio, we felt it was justified for the first run of the course on the basis that both tutors needed to learn from each other's practice in the process of developing the course. In the first instance we would need plenty of opportunity to reflect upon how the group was working, how we were each contributing, and what the educational values were that were emerging from our practice. We both came to the project from different perspectives in terms of our fields of research and our teaching experience. Working together, as well as working with the group, was clearly to be a learning and research process for us both. Future courses were organized as two parallel groups of ten, each with one tutor, but we felt justified in pooling our resources fully at this first stage in the course's life.

The course was constructed around four, termly modules followed by a period of independent work towards a dissertation. The meetings for each module were built around initial and final conference days (just before and after each academic term, when lecturers are under less pressure to teach), and five, fortnightly, afternoon meetings during term time. Between meetings all participants would be expected to make observations and interpretations of their own teaching, try out different strategies in the light of these and thereby develop their own ongoing projects. In the initial stages of the course at least, we envisaged that we might need to provide some guidance on how to set about this process. As the course proceeded, however, we hoped that individuals would develop their own characteristic lines of enquiry, which would be the subject of constructive critique by the group.

With this emphasis on the participants pursuing their own lines of enquiry arising from their practice and interests, it was nevertheless important for the group to have some sense of a unified task and purpose. The structure for this was to be provided by aims that were encompassed by all the modules, and also the themes identified for each module. In practice, the cohesiveness of the group was also reinforced by a number of principles. Some of these have been suggested by the discussion above; others were only to emerge in a tentative fashion as the meetings of the course progressed.

It is important to stress here that we saw the aims of the course as applying to us, the course tutors, as well as to the participants. This was necessary if we were to learn alongside the rest of the group. It meant that we had to resist the temptation to hide behind our tutorly status and assumptions about our own expertise, and recognize our own need for development in these areas.

These were the aims, on which I shall comment briefly here in the light of the discussion in Chapters 1 and 2, returning to them later in the light of subsequent evaluation of the programme:

- *To make practice public* This involves developing our abilities as observers of our own practice, writing about it, interpreting it and sharing reflections with each other. This reflection upon practice would form a basis in experience from which theoretical ideas might emerge and practices change. As teaching is subjected to increasing control through quality audit arrangements, it is vital that the actual experience of teachers, rather than the agendas of auditors, administrators and politicians, provides the basis for a developing language and conceptualization of teaching processes.
- *To understand how our students perceive their learning experience and the subject matter* Without such understanding, any change in teaching methods lacks foundation. What we can discover of their perspective is valuable research evidence. This research attitude demands that we consider the role of teaching to be one of listening at least as much as one of speaking: that

teaching is a two-way process of communication, and that what students have to say about their learning is always most significant. Such an approach is to be contrasted with the normal student feedback questionnaires that have now become an integral part of the quality control machinery. As current research indicates (Johnson 1998), these questionnaires are often seen by students as limiting, rather than enhancing, genuine communication between teachers and students. Their purpose has more to do with the technology of control than with the development of communication and understanding between teachers and learners. Coming to understand the students' experience demands a more sustained dialogue between teachers and learners.

- *To develop the educational values* Values lie at the heart of our educational practice. It was therefore important for us all to attempt to make them open to critique by the group. The application of teaching methods depends upon professional judgements made in the light of educational values. While some (for example Winter and Maisch 1996) see the ability to articulate such values and make judgements in the light of them as a fundamental aspect of professional competence, too often the notion of skills and competence are viewed as value-free technical attributes. In this course we wanted to resist this tendency; otherwise, our teaching is likely to develop merely as an instrument of external agendas based upon non-educational values (such as those of the market place), which are outside our control.

- *To develop a research community* In the first instance this community was the course group itself. As the course continued, however, with new participants joining in future years, the idea was that this community might become a network across the institution. While participants of the group would offer support for ongoing research and testing new ideas for teaching we also needed to explore how such a community might relate to developments within departments, and how the wider university context might support or constrain the development of this collegial approach. We envisaged that, over time, a network of present and past participants would continue to offer this kind of support.

- *To relate teaching to research* The potential for drawing teaching and research into a closer relationship in our own institution was indicated by the study reported in Chapter 2. Bearing in mind the conflicting pressures that people face to increase research output while teaching larger numbers of students, the course intended to realize this potential. This was to be, perhaps, the biggest challenge for the course.

- *To develop strategies for self-evaluation* 'Student-centred learning', which the representatives from EHE wanted to promote through their support of the course, involves, among other things, students having a greater responsibility for their own learning and a greater role in its assessment. Such an approach, we considered, could not only be justified on educational grounds, but could also help to give students a more influential voice within the institution.

We saw these aims as suggesting a kind of research agenda that would apply throughout our work together. The actual content within which they would be addressed would emerge from the interests of the group and their developing enquiries. Provisionally, however, we provided a framework of one theme, which provided the title for each of the four modules: Group Work; Assessment; Curriculum Design; and Active Learning. For each we indicated the kind of issues that might emerge within these themes. While we did not see this as a prescription, we felt it was important for us to prepare some resources (such as readings and activities) that could be drawn upon as the work developed.

Such module titles may seem to contradict the emphasis we have placed upon reflection, values and critique; suggestive of a course more concerned with teaching technique than we intended. The reasons for this discrepancy are not, however, accidental. It must be borne in mind that the context for the course was one in which current discourses of teaching in higher education, as in schools and colleges, had recently begun to be dominated by technical rather than critical perspectives. By using titles that had a currency within this dominant discourse, we wished to re-appropriate these notions within a framework that gave more space for the exploration of educational values in practice. Significantly, once the course had been established for two years, we changed the titles of the modules to: The Social Nature of Learning; Assessment; The Curriculum; and The Role of the Teacher. These titles more accurately reflected our design for a more widely conceived course.

Exploring the process

Selecting a group of 12 from the 21 applications was not easy. We assumed that everyone was equally able to take part and gain from the course so we did not hold interviews. Instead, we aimed to form a group that represented a cross-section of disciplines and a wide range of lecturing experience. We wanted women to be well represented on the course. (There were no non-white applicants to this initial course.) We also insisted that prospective participants should, as far as possible, free themselves to attend all sessions and, initially at least, have every intention of completing the course as far as the Masters level.

Upon this basis we selected the group, offering all those who were unsuccessful a first option on the second course, which we aimed to start a year later.

With the wide range of prior experience represented in the group, an immediate problem for us was to 'match' what we provided to their needs. This became very clear to us during the second meeting when, among other things, the group discussed two readings that we had suggested as possibly providing a basic orientation to research that we would be promoting on this course. One of these was roundly criticized by many in the group as being written in language that was inaccessible to them, while some who claimed to have fewer problems with the language said that it was saying nothing new. The other reading was thought by some to be naïve, and by others to be underpinned by a political viewpoint that they did not share. Later readings during the course were received more favourably, but what seemed to strike a chord with some people was rejected by others.

This suggested to us that we needed to be clear about the place of readings in the course. They were to provide an opportunity for criticism, a perspective against which people could try out their own ideas, rather than a basic knowledge that the course aimed to 'teach'. During the four modules of the course, the place of these readings changed. As concerns, interests, and the language in which to talk about them became shared among the group, participants were more ready to provide sources of written material that they had found interesting. As this happened, readings became more of a resource to draw on than a set unifying element. I remember how, in the final module, a major text suggested by the tutors was responded to enthusiastically by the group, who were then dismayed to learn that both tutors were highly critical of the text. This led to valuable discussion of how a text can be of considerable value even if one is very critical of what it is saying.

But while reading might inform practice, it was to be people's actual teaching experience that would provide the basis for development. The problem then was to structure our time together in such a way as to give everyone a chance to bring their own ideas about their teaching, and the results of their research on it, to the group for consideration. The danger was that unless we provided adequate opportunity for particular projects to be considered in some detail, we would simply deal with all issues at a superficial level, merely rehearsing our preconceived viewpoints rather than exploring their application to actual practices. On the other hand, within the limitations of time, each participant could not expect to receive the group's concentrated attention on their projects for very long.

We soon centred our two-hour meetings on a form that involved people taking it in turns to decide what they wanted to do for half the session. Sometimes this would be an account of a course of work being planned, at others a small-scale piece of research they had done into their students' perceptions of their learning. Occasionally the participants would bring into the group a few students, who would talk about how they experienced their teaching, or a representative from a professional body, who would address the issue of what they thought should be the aims of a professional course. Or perhaps someone would bring to the group no more than a subject for discussion. In later modules, even this degree of structuring was seen to be an unnecessary artificiality in the emerging process.

In this way, our meetings were increasingly determined by the participants. By the final module we, the tutors, were no longer required to structure the process or the content of the sessions. If someone felt the quality of discussion was limited in some way, or that we were not addressing what was important, then they were usually able to say that was how they felt so that the group could do something about it. Responsibility thus became widely shared and we had, to this extent, succeeded in becoming a research forum, rather than merely a taught course.

In order to arrive at this point, however, one principle had emerged to be important from an early stage in the group's meetings. This was the idea that we might use our shared experience of the course as an instance of educational practice to be reflected upon. For example, at one point in the first module we were interested in pursuing the issue of how people in a teaching group perceive power relationships in the group, and how these impinge upon their ability to contribute. Such an issue is of general significance in group work. It was therefore useful to reflect upon how relationships of power were perceived by us in our own group, comparing and contrasting our perceptions in order to provide an experiential basis to our developing ideas about power in group settings. Similarly, questions about assessment led the group to question the assessment procedures of this course; curriculum design issues were related to our design for our work together. Almost any general issue about teaching could be related to how we were operating within this shared educational setting.

While this strategy enabled us to build our understanding on the one educational practice we shared – our work together – it was based on an assumption that ideas gained from analysis of this setting could usefully be transferred into the wide variety of teaching scenarios in which the participants worked. We recognized, however, that making this transfer is no easy matter. We came from a wide variety of teaching contexts, each of which offered constraints as well as opportunities for making use of the understandings gained during the course.

Although the participants appeared to think that this assumption of transferability was valid much of the time, there were aspects of our work together that, they felt, were significantly different from their learning contexts with their students. For example, smaller numbers were involved in this course than in much of their undergraduate teaching. Furthermore, the status differential between Len and myself and the participants was generally thought to be less than that between the participants and their students. The significance of such differences is, however, open to question. They may make transference difficult, but not impossible.

This reflexive approach also challenged Len and me to be explicit about why we had organized the course the way we had, and why we intervened in the ways we did. If the group was to be the subject of critical reflection, then so was our practice as tutors within it. This is not always a comfortable position to be in. But since the aim of the course was for us to engage together in rethinking our ideas about teaching, we had to be a part of that learning process and submit ourselves to the kind of scrutiny we expected of the other participants.

Writing to enquire

During each module participants were encouraged to keep a research diary of observations and interpretations they had made of an aspect of their teaching; accounts of their thinking in response to the discussions of the group; critical responses to any of the literature encountered; evaluative comments about the course itself, and so on.

These were private documents to which no one else, including the tutors, had any rights of access. The material from them might be used in informal seminars on the course, or it might be used as a basis for later publications, or to identify issues that require further exploration with other participants or the course tutors.

The research diaries would also be a major source of material for compiling a portfolio of work relating to each module. Assessment on the 'taught' element of the course was solely on the basis of these portfolios, which were to be submitted following each module's completion, and assessed on a pass/fail basis with an opportunity to resubmit if that seemed appropriate. A more important aspect of assessment, however, was the opportunity it provided for the tutors to provide detailed written responses, which would then be developed in personal tutorial sessions. In this way, assessment was seen as part of the ongoing dialogue of teaching and researching the emerging themes. The criteria for assessing portfolios included the preparedness of the participant to take risks in both their practice of teaching and in their interpretation. For many this seemed strange: the culture of academic writing often allows little space for risk taking and speculation, but emphasizes instead proof and certainty. We found that once people felt free to write in more tentative and imaginative ways, doors were more readily opened to new ideas and practices.

We were concerned that these portfolios should be seen as working documents, as tools for thinking through ideas about practice, rather than as final products. We were aware that as the course got under way, and as we found out more about the individual projects through personal tutorials, clarity might be gained about how they might best be constructed. What seemed to be of more immediate importance, however, was that participants should see their own regular writing to be a fundamental part of the enquiry process.

Writing in such a way as to explore the professional values that underlie practice is not easy. Such values are always difficult to express. Their articulation needs to be retraced as they become questioned and new experience is brought to bear on them. Thus we would expect the participants to refine, in one portfolio, ideas that may have initially been raised in an earlier one. They would pursue themes of enquiry across consecutive portfolios, constantly reviewing and clarifying their values and how these can be realized in practice.

Portfolio writing was also to prepare the participants for writing a dissertation in which these emerging issues could be investigated in more depth.

This document would report a more extended piece of research and present it in a form more appropriate for a public audience, with some attempt to relate it to a wider field of educational thinking.

These initial considerations of the importance of writing in the professional development of the participants were extended in the subsequent years of the course. At this early stage what became clear to us was that more creative approaches to writing could play an important part in the exploration of values, and how these can be more adequately understood and reflected in the practice of teaching.

Through such a research orientation to our practice as teachers, we became aware of the enormous complexities involved in attempting to build real progress. These complexities concern not only processes of teaching and learning but also the web of institutional structures that symbolize and reinforce current practices and relationships. These difficulties are not amenable to short term solutions. They demand a constant challenge and struggle if we are to take teaching seriously.

Acknowledging values such as these immediately leads us to having to confront certain dilemmas in our teaching. How can we genuinely collaborate with those (our students) over whom we have institutionalized power? How can we adequately discover and value the knowledge our students bring in the light of our own greater expertise? How are we to take account of such distorting influences as class, gender, disability and race when we, ourselves, are shaped by the same social forces? Such questions – and there are many others – emerge as soon as we attempt to articulate our practice of teaching in the light of the social context in which it takes place. They are questions that will remain unasked as long as the development of teaching is viewed merely as the development of method and skill. In this course we attempted to generate an environment in which such questions can be asked and enquired into in direct relation to our own teaching.

To return to Chris, the lecturer whose comments opened this book, such questioning makes things difficult. We cannot continue to teach in the same way. But at the same time it opens up an arena for investigation to which we can apply the very abilities that brought us to work in a university in the first place: the aptitude for sustained reflection and critical investigation. Only by applying these can we give expression to the values that inform our teaching and confront the social pressures that aim to reduce practice to the mere application of technique.

Evaluating the outcomes

In his review of different approaches to educational development, Gosling suggests that the approach we have adopted on this course may well 'take a critical stance towards the institution, its strategy and its policies . . . [and] is unlikely to be the model of educational development endorsed by university managements' (Gosling 1997: 214).

This comment might seem to be confirmed by those of several students on the course, who have said that they cannot understand why the university funds the course. 'Does the Vice-chancellor really know what we are doing?' has been said to me on more than one occasion, in the light of discussions at which university policies, structures or practices have been questioned.

Such comments are, I believe, the result of an over-simplification. I have argued that the university teacher's enquiry should take a critical stance towards the institutional and wider social constraints that shape their practices. This does not mean, however, that we are unable to create real change that is valued by management, nor does it mean that a critical stance is not viable in this context, for two reasons.

First, institutional life is more complex than these comments suggest, and is often contradictory. One of the contradictions of the traditional university resides in its rhetoric of critical and independent thought, which lies alongside instrumentally managerialist practices and market values. A course like the one I have described may fit uncomfortably alongside managerialism and marketization, but it resonates well with the rhetoric of critical, or at least liberal, thinking which is reflected in the investigation into teaching and research reported in Chapter 2.

Second, a course that is constructed along these lines – with its emphasis on the teacher's processes of critical enquiry – will subject institutional practices and policies to critique. But it may *also* be as effective, or more effective, than a more skills oriented course, in producing the kinds of outcomes that the institution wants: able and thoughtful teachers.

Reviewing the course after it had been running for seven years, we have sought to test both of these assertions: has the course had an impact at an institutional level, and has it led to a development of the individual participants' practices? These are the questions to which I shall now turn.

The development of the course over eight years was supported by an ongoing process of evaluative research and collaboration among the teaching team, the participants and colleagues from other institutions. What I want to draw upon here, however, is the kind of evaluative question which was of most interest to the university. That is, to put it crudely, has the course produced definable outcomes in terms of developing staff and the quality of learning?

After the course had been running for three years it seemed important to be able to answer this. I asked the university's assistant registrar, rather than the course team, to conduct this evaluation based upon the aims of the course. His evaluation would, I reasoned, be more readily seen as representing the university's interests, and be undistorted by the particular concerns of those of us who designed and taught on the programme. We would have no part in devising whatever questions might be asked of present or past participants or the collection or analysis of any data.

This led, in 1995, to a survey of all present and past participants, based upon a questionnaire. The survey was repeated in 1998 using the same

questionnaire, to which over 60 per cent of the 78 past and present participants responded. These have provided concrete evidence that the course has
contributed to institutional change and professional development. The ways
in which it does this will be considered in later chapters. Here I want to
concentrate on general outcomes.

Changes in teaching methods

Almost everyone was able to identify specific ways in which their teaching
had changed. These changes were often expressed in such terms as: 'less
didactic, more student centred'; 'more innovative lecturing methods'; 'more
experiential and cooperative learning'; 'greater student involvement'. To
some extent these changes were the result of people developing specific
techniques, such as regular student evaluation, small group work, project
and problem based learning or the use of some new technology, but
often changes in teaching were felt to be the result of increased awareness: 'it challenged the traditional way of learning'; 'it gave me more confidence in surrendering power to students'; 'more aware of the student as
learner'.

It is significant that these responses were very much in line with the kinds
of developments in teaching that EHE, the original proposers for the course,
had in mind. Thus, while we did not see the development of skills and
techniques as being the primary focus of the course (but rather the ability
to investigate one's teaching), they were nevertheless important outcomes.
This would seem to confirm the principle that I suggested in Chapter 1,
that an approach that focuses on enquiry into one's teaching leads directly
to improved teaching.

Changes in assessment

Again, a range of specific new methods were indicated – portfolio based
assessment, peer assessment, report based continuous assessment, oral presentations, and so on – almost all of which placed the learner in a more
central role in the assessment of their learning.

Changes in curriculum content

Here the findings were not quite so clear. Two-thirds of the respondents
identified specific changes, and these, like the changes in methods, usually
involved giving the students a greater role in shaping their curriculum. A
significant number of more junior colleagues, however, felt powerless to
effect significant change in the curriculum. My own experience of tutoring

the course would suggest that this dissatisfaction might be even greater than the survey indicated. Participants quite often complain that they have all sorts of ideas about what they want to change, but feel powerless to do anything about it. This serves to emphasize that the improvement of student learning is not only a matter of individuals developing their abilities, but requires changes at departmental and institutional levels as well. Some indication of the extent to which this might have been achieved may be gained from a measure of the course participants' involvement in the university's quality enhancement activities.

Involvement in quality enhancement activities

Over two-thirds of the people who had completed the course had increased their involvement in quality enhancement activities at departmental, faculty and university levels. Many also identified less formal ways in which they had contributed to changes beyond their own teaching. While one might be sceptical that involvement in the bureaucratic machinery of quality enhancement really improves the students' experience of learning, there is no doubt that such mechanisms are more likely to be helpful if those involved in such committees and groups have a serious commitment to educational enquiry. Just as significant in contributing to change, however, might be the comment of a number of people who said that they were much more confident to speak up on teaching matters and influence their colleagues at a national as well as local level.

Influence on research

Over 70 per cent of the respondents said that the course had influenced their research. For most of these, reference was made to *educational* research, rather than research in their own discipline. This included publications in 15 different educational journals, chapters in books, and even whole books produced by the participants. Such an outcome was to be expected. More interesting, however, were comments made on how the course, with its focus on teaching and learning, influenced their own discipline based research.

These comments included: 'I became much more interested in the human/societal impact of technology (my research field)'; 'have begun to study journal articles in various disciplines in an attempt to see how authors were taught'; 'heightened my interest and awareness of areas of research'; 'transferred research skills learned on the course to a history project'; 'more interested in how students acquire research skills'. Such comments indicate a broadening of research interest. This is consistent with the suggestion in the study described in Chapter 2, that a broader approach to disciplinary research related more closely to an interest in teaching.

Impact upon career enhancement

This is inevitably difficult to measure. Many people said that they could not be sure of the extent to which their participation in the course had contributed to some advancement they had achieved. Furthermore, a significant number of those who did not respond to the survey were people with whom we had lost contact after they had moved on to other institutions. Presumably, most of these would have been moves to better posts. For this reason, the figure of a third of participants who said that their participation had led to an improved position is likely to be an underestimate.

Nevertheless, two people were able to identify conclusively that their involvement was the most important factor in gaining a promoted position at another institution, a further three or four felt that it was an important factor in obtaining promotion, and a much larger group said that it had led to an improved role without promotion.

Problems and possibilities

It is, of course, a common complaint that teaching is not accorded an adequately high status in academic life. This has been acknowledged by policy discussion documents in the UK, such as the Dearing Report (NCIHE 1997), and the Institute of Learning and Teaching aims to address it (ILTPG 1998: 3). It should be borne in mind, however, that this survey related to a period of time that largely preceded such documents, and to an 'old' university, whose reputation has been built mainly on its research achievements. In the light of this, the effects of the course upon career enhancement are encouraging. Perhaps there is a danger in being too pessimistic about the undervaluing of teaching, even in narrow career terms. A research or enquiry approach to its development can contribute to career advancement even though, as Gosling warns us (Gosling 1997: 214), such an approach involves taking a critical stance towards one's own institutional policies and practices.

A survey that aims to identify 'positive indicators' of performance is unlikely to reflect the subtlety of professional change. As several participants commented in their questionnaires, they could not quantify the effects. Nevertheless, it did provide us with some strong confirmation that the course had indeed both led to a development of individuals' teaching, and to some departmental change.

Although the survey was designed largely to identify positive outcomes of the course, rather than problems, a number of comments confirmed more anecdotal evidence concerning the difficulties of giving serious enquiry into teaching an important role. The course has always received unreserved support and funding from the university's senior managers and administrators. There were several participants, however, who felt that their contribution to it was not valued by their heads of department. More than one was told that this was an interest that they should pursue 'in their spare time'; others said that such work was considered in the department to be a distraction from their 'real' research; and one or two others felt that such involvement would be unlikely to lead to promotion. I have also been told stories of how the department offered little support or recognition of the participant's involvement until it came to the time when it was assessed by the teaching quality assurance (TQA) exercise. Then there appeared to be a sudden interest and cynical attempt to make sure staff involvement was mentioned in all the appropriate documentation.

With these kinds of problem in mind, it is important to recognize the extent to which the programme requires staff time in addition to their normal work load. In a section of the survey that allowed for further comments, many respondents spoke of the quality of this time: the kind of space that the course provided was quite different from their other work experience. The quality of this space for enquiry is the subject of the ensuing chapters. Here I shall simply draw upon some of the comments made.

Most of these comments referred to a different way of thinking about their work: 'it forced me to think about all sorts of concepts which one either took for granted or did not even consider'; 'It changed the way I think about things – both personal and professional'; 'aware of a far wider landscape'; 'revealed the complexity and problems in what I once considered as safe territory'.

These changes were often related to the space for reflection that the course provided. Two qualities of this 'space' were identified in these comments. One was that the space allowed people to pursue their own investigations in, as one put it, 'a non-didactic environment'. Another was the value participants placed upon working alongside colleagues from different disciplinary backgrounds. In all of the course evaluations over seven years, this has perhaps been the most consistent comment.

But what is a 'space of enquiry' or a 'non-didactic environment'? How is it that working with colleagues from different backgrounds can promote our understanding of teaching and learning? Is there some kind of educational theory that accounts for the value of these qualities, or helps us to analyse them or design activity that promotes them? Indeed, does educationa' theory have a role to play in developing the university teacher's enquiry? These are the questions I shall turn to in Chapter 4.

4

A Pedagogical Theory?

Introduction

It may not be long before all university lecturers will have to demonstrate that they are competent to teach. Many universities in the Western world already have in place programmes, including certificated courses, that are designed to prepare them for this. Some of these are compulsory for all new lecturers, some voluntary.

In the UK, the ILT in higher education was set up in 1999. One of its tasks is to accredit courses, programmes and 'pathways' that would provide professional development programmes in university teaching for academic staff. In the process of consultation for the ILT, recommendations were made concerning how such courses might be accredited and what they might aim to achieve (Booth 1998). A great deal of emphasis has been placed on how teachers might demonstrate their competence to teach, and prescriptions have been indicated about how portfolios of evidence should be constructed (ILT 1999) for this purpose, but very little is said about how academics taking part in a programme might actually learn about teaching.

Chapter 3 described a course, at Masters level, that provides a context for exploring how teachers might learn about teaching from each other. The programme was for academics with varying degrees of experience in teaching. Only about a quarter of all participants had less than two years' experience. It soon became very clear to us that the more experienced teachers had much to learn from those with less experience, as well as vice versa. But what kind of processes might take place when university teachers work together to develop their educational understanding and practice? How might they draw upon their own and each other's disciplinary understanding? What kind of knowledge might be involved? What kind of enquiry or investigation might be involved in generating this knowledge? To pose the question more generally, what kind of pedagogical theory might underlie the process of learning about teaching for academics?

Unless those who provide such programmes can begin to answer this question, it is difficult to see how we are likely to achieve the envisaged development of university teaching. Indeed, overcoming the public perception that university teaching is 'amateurish' (Booth 1998: 1) demands that the processes of developing it be adequately conceptualized.

I shall consider the question 'what pedagogical theory underlies the course described in Chapter 3?' in two ways. First, to understand what the question really means: to try and 'deconstruct' it; and second, to attempt to answer it by drawing upon the course and the perspective that I have developed so far in the preceding chapters.

What kind of question is this?

What would count as an answer to such a question? I might, for example, respond by saying: 'The pedagogy of the course is based upon Rogerian principles of facilitation'; or alternatively, 'The curriculum of the course is underpinned by critical theory'; or 'Kolb's learning cycle provides the basis for our work' (Kolb 1984). On the face of it, such responses look like possible answers to the question. Each indicates a theoretical framework that can be referenced through a literature. Such an eclectic response might be useful, particularly to those new to teaching.

As soon as we look more closely at such theoretical resources, however, this kind of answer seems less satisfactory, or rather, somewhat incomplete. It is incomplete because the question 'Why Rogerian?' or 'Why critical theory?' should surely be a legitimate question on any course that is educational. I cannot imagine that the academics who took part in the course described in Chapter 3 would have *failed* to ask such questions. In other words, it would seem to be a condition of a course *in* education that any theoretical perspective it offers is open to question or *critique*.

No theory, however, can be critiqued from within its own axioms or assumptions. This is the paradox of metatheory. As soon as we ask: 'Why adopt this theory rather than that one?' our answer involves us making a judgement, which must be based upon yet another theory: a metatheory. In its most general form, this is the perhaps unsurprising assertion that the validity of reason cannot be demonstrated by reasoning, since any such demonstration would presuppose the validity of the thing whose validity one is seeking to demonstrate. (For an intriguing book woven around this and related themes, see Hofstadter 1979). This problem was also the starting point to Descartes's First Meditation (Descartes 1960) in the seventeenth century. He wondered whether he could really be certain about anything, and that perhaps some kind of 'demon' was even tricking him into believing his senses and his powers of reason. In the Second Meditation, he had the insight that since he was thinking about the problem, at least he could be sure of his own existence, since there must be something that was doing this thinking: *cogito ergo sum.*

While such philosophical considerations should not detain us here, it is worth noting that this search for certainty is often a problem for academics who come to consider educational theory for the first time. It also continues to be a problem for philosophers. Postmodernists, such as Rorty (1982), have drawn our attention to the impossibility of any absolute theoretical justification. He would even go further to argue, contrary to Descartes, that reason itself is relative to a particular group of people who share certain cultural features: an intersubjective community. In practice, such an idea does not seem to be altogether fanciful when academics from different disciplines start to discuss the different ways of thinking that underlie their own subject.

Returning to the question of the theoretical basis for a curriculum for developing teaching and learning, this problem is easiest to see in the case of critical theory. This is a theoretical perspective that shows how truth and rationality (which are necessary for learning) are distorted unless communication is democratic (Carr 1995: 12). This clearly has implications for how students and teachers should relate, but if a course is *based* upon critical theory, then either such theory is assumed and unquestioned (which would be uncritical) or else it is open to critique from some perspective outside critical theory, in which case critical theory's status as being the underlying theory for the course is called into question.

So far this argument suggests that the question 'what is the underlying theory of the course?' may be based upon a misleading assumption that an educational course should be based upon a theory. Alternatively, the question is really asking for something rather different. Let us assume, for the moment, the latter and suggest what else might be required in responding to this question.

One possibility is that the question is not looking for an 'underlying theory' but rather 'a set of theoretical resources or insights'. Now this seems to me to be a very different sort of question. For it acknowledges that a curriculum can be open to different interpretations. There is not one overarching theory that draws it together, but rather a more pluralistic or eclectic range of insights, methods, approaches, and so on. Viewing the question in this way, I might respond that the course draws upon Rogerian insights regarding the facilitation process, critical theory in terms of an awareness of power relationships and democracy, and Kolb's learning cycle in terms of the value of reflection in the learning process.

Now this is beginning to look like an erudite kind of answer to the question. It presents us with a problem though, for although one might usefully draw upon all of these perspectives (and many others), only a little understanding of each of these 'theories' indicates that in many respects each one contradicts elements of the other two. But then making professional judgements often involves confronting conflicting theories and values. This is why we face the kind of professional dilemmas that are a recurring theme as we enquire into our teaching.

There is, however, another intention that often lies behind this question of an underlying theory. This concerns academic credibility. This is of particular significance to educational development (or academic development, or staff development) workers, who are often viewed by their colleagues in disciplinary departments as not being 'real academics'. The work of such 'developers' is often seen as merely practical and lacking in theoretical underpinnings.

Roughly interpreted, the intention behind the question posed in this context might be: 'On what basis can you persuade me that this is an *academic* course and that you have the intellectual resources required to teach it?' Now a question like this is political and not just about intellectual abilities. How we are to respond to it depends upon our understanding of the political context in which it is asked. For example, in a climate in which academic staff are suspicious of attempts to force prescriptive training programmes upon them, such questions might be pursued in order to cast doubt upon their intellectual merit.

Often when I have been asked the question, I have felt – and have had good reason to believe – that this is the spirit in which the question is intended. If it is one's credibility as an academic that is at stake in being asked this question, then it is important to find out as much as possible about the status of the interlocutor, their disciplinary and theoretical background and their particular interest in the course. The following fieldnote is an instance of my attempt to deal with this problem. It arises from my work on an academic link programme overseas.

Fieldnote 1

I was visiting a university in another country to support some colleagues who were proposing to mount a course along the lines of the Sheffield Masters course. They wanted me to speak on their behalf to a senior academic whom they understood to be quite hostile – on academic grounds – to the proposal and likely to block its passage through various committees. Before the meeting I found out from one of my colleagues that he was a Dean of Theology, with a background in classics and philosophy. My colleague considered him to have a generally conservative disposition towards educational innovation, but nevertheless a genial manner. With this knowledge, I could judge that during my discussions outlining the course proposal, it might be helpful to talk about the course in terms with which he had some familiarity.

One aspect of the course that was very important to us was the close relationship that it envisages between theory and practice. Now someone with a background in classical philosophy would be familiar with debates around the question of the relationship between practice and theory. While the Platonic conception is that theory represents a kind of perfection, which practice only more or less imitates, the Aristotelian conception is that theory and practice mutually inform each other (see Carr 1995: 67–8 for a helpful commentary on this). This is an important aspect of the course, since we do not aim to teach educational theory that is then to be applied (which might be a Platonic approach), but rather to reflect upon our own practice of teaching with the aim of developing theories that may then go on to inform future practice (a more Aristotelian approach).

To enter the discussion with some reference to the roots of this idea in Aristotle's writing enabled me to signify to the Dean of Theology that I wanted to engage with respect to his disciplinary background. I could, alternatively, have initiated my account in terms of 'student-centred learning', or 'multidisciplinarity', or by appealing to a liberal notion of scholarship. All such approaches would have been honest and helpful. But my choice of the theory–practice relationship as a way into the discussion was chosen because it related to his discourse. By acknowledging the relevance of his own disciplinary background, I was entitled to membership of his academic language community and therefore I, and more importantly the course that I was advocating, would be entitled to be given academic respect.

Of course, this strategy was risky. Had the Dean cross-examined me on Aristotle's theory I would surely have been found wanting. I was not presuming, however, to be an expert in his discipline but simply to acknowledge its value. On later reflection, it seemed clear to me that it was largely as a result of my preparedness to bridge what might have been a disciplinary divide between us that led to his subsequent support for the course proposal.

This strategy does not always work. At times it has led me into embarrassing situations where my own ignorance is made apparent. But I have two other reasons for giving this account here.

First, I wish to make a distinction (not always an easy one to make in practice) between the explicit question about the theoretical basis of a course (or curriculum, or research methodology), and an implicit question motivated by a concern to establish academic credentials within a context of often oppressive power relationships. In other words I am trying to distinguish between the political and the intellectual agendas underlying such a question. I am aware that such a distinction is somewhat problematic, since what counts as 'intellectual' is also highly shaped by political forces. Nevertheless, in a particular political context, this distinction in terms of motives can, I believe, be made.

Second, the fieldnote illustrates a very real problem in attempting to persuade someone who thinks within one paradigm (or theoretical framework) of the validity of an alternative one. Indeed, in order to communicate with him, perhaps I had little alternative but to attempt to speak in a language with which he was familiar. I was not deceiving him about the importance of Aristotle's philosophy to our course, but merely initiating discussions from a shared reference point.

In Chapter 1 I suggested that we should be cautious about viewing questions about teaching and learning as if they were generic; that is, as if they were independent of any particular discipline. In Fieldnote 1, I described my attempt to communicate the credibility of a course by introducing it in terms of the Dean's own discipline. If we continually emphasize the generic nature of teaching and learning by refusing to engage with particular disciplinary perspectives, we inevitably reinforce the prejudice that matters of teaching and learning are 'merely' practical questions of no intellectual interest. The prevalence of this prejudiced view in academic life continually undermines the value of teaching.

Levels of theory

There is another difficulty with trying to respond to questions about a theory that might underlie a course. What *counts* as a theory is not clear. For a certain kind of psychologist, 'Kolb's learning cycle' might count as a possible theory for explaining how participants learn. A different kind of psychologist, say a Skinnerian, would acknowledge that Kolb's theory is a theory, but that it is wrong, or at least incomplete. A Marxist, on the other hand, may say that it is not even a theory, merely a model perhaps, because it refuses even to consider the ways in which such terms as 'reflection' and 'learning' derive their meaning from social relationships of power.

So we seem to have different levels of theory here: theories that might be contested on the basis that they provide contradictory explanations of the same kinds of phenomena; and theories that are unable to compete, not because they relate to a different subject matter, but because they pay attention to different features of the subject matter. Let me give an example taken directly from the Masters course described in Chapter 3.

Fieldnote 2

During one session of the course, six lecturers were sitting in a circle, with me as the tutor, at the beginning of a module of work on assessment in higher education. One of them said that if we want to assess learning, we first have to agree what learning is. 'What is learning?'

A microbiologist who specialized in the brain said: 'Well, learning is about what happens in the brain. If we really understood about synapses and the sequence and conditions in which they were activated, we would, in principle, know how learning takes place and whether it has taken place'.

A psychologist disagreed: 'What we really need to understand is the chemical changes that take place. If we knew these we would be able to establish that learning had taken place'.

A psychoanalyst responded: 'That's nothing to do with it. It's much more a matter of how the individual is influenced by early childhood

---

relationships, especially with parents, and how the various complexes
that arise are resolved'.

The next, a sociologist, said: 'What really matters is an individual's
social location in terms of class, gender, ethnicity, and so on. If we
could precisely define these things then we would have a good idea as
to what influences learning'.

I imagined that, had the philosopher, who was away on that day,
been present, she might have commented: 'It all depends what you
mean by learning.'

The group view me as an educationalist, I think. I said nothing.

Although not recorded until some time after the events, this fieldnote is
almost word for word what took place. What was happening here? What
'theories' were being indicated and at what level? Should I, as the 'facilitator'
(I do not like the term) have had some kind of metatheory, or 'educational' theory, that could somehow draw upon these different and perhaps
contradictory contributions? How might this kind of discussion develop in
such a way as to enhance the participants' understanding and practice of
teaching?

Broadly, there seem to be three different ways in which the above exchange
might be developed, each of which would reflect a different underlying
theory of the course (and the tutor's 'facilitation' of it).

The first approach might be to move away from these somewhat 'philosophical' questions about the nature of learning; to acknowledge instead
that we share a concern for the same practical task of teaching; and to see
the aim of the course as being the development of teaching techniques.
Such an approach views the issue as being generic. Following this approach,
while it might be recognized that different techniques might be appropriate in different subject contexts, the participants are encouraged to 'leave
outside the door' their frameworks of disciplinary thinking, and address
themselves directly to the questions of how to teach. This approach is *technical*, and not concerned with theoretical or disciplinary perspectives. The
potential contradiction arising from differing theories would then be avoided
altogether.

The second approach would, like the first, largely set aside the disciplinary
frameworks of thinking of the participants, and thus be generic. It would
view the educational task, however, as not merely technical or practical. It
would concern itself with *educational theory*. In other words, participants would
be invited to engage in a form of theorizing and a body of theory that would,
for some at least, be quite new to them. This approach may be 'critical' or
'practical' in a variety of ways, depending on the nature of the educational
theory employed. It will be theoretical and disciplinary, within the *discipline*
of education. In relation to such an approach, the question 'What is the
underlying theory?' would seem to be quite appropriate and would invite a
response in terms of a theory within the discipline of education. With this

approach, the contradictions that arise from the different disciplinary frameworks of theory would be avoided. If contradiction were now encountered, this would be within the discipline of *educational theory*.

Neither of these approaches, however, really draws upon the kinds of contribution the participants might make if they were to pursue their thinking further along the lines initiated in Fieldnote 2. Drawing upon the disciplinary insights offered here, the participants might be encouraged to consider: the kinds of values involved in these different positions; the ways in which each could offer a challenge to the others; and the ways in which each discipline might – from its different theoretical framework – offer its own critique of the others. An approach such as this would be critical, but not critical from within a discipline; rather it would be a form of critical interdisciplinarity. Barnett (1990: 165) argues that some such form of critical interdisciplinarity should play at least some part in all students' experience of higher education. What is suggested here is that lecturers, like their students, should also gain from this critical approach in relation to their own teaching. From this approach, the potential for contradiction would emerge immediately as participants began to explore the different values and assumptions underlying their disciplines.

It is this third approach that most closely relates to the context of the Masters programme at Sheffield, and is the basis for the enquiring university teacher as I understand it. Starting from this point, the original question 'What is the underlying theory of the course?' now becomes more like 'How does the course draw upon the theories of the participants?' What is interdisciplinarity? Is it fundamentally contradictory?

Interdisciplinarity

My colleagues in Fieldnote 2 were not in debate in an important sense. They were not trying to contest each other's theory, although what they each had to say was an expression of their particular theoretical perspective. As the discussion developed, they became increasingly fascinated in how quite different 'stories' can be told of the same thing – learning. At one level they seemed to be saying contradictory things. Or were they perhaps not talking about the 'same' thing?

In a sense, of course, they were telling stories about very different things: about parental relationships, or neurones firing, or social class. But each was speaking about learning. The danger is that it is easy to be misled into thinking that learning is a 'thing'. So-called 'educational theories' are often referred to as though they deal with learning as if it were an object like a brick or a bridge. For example, Kolb's learning cycle (Kolb 1984) is often used as if this process of reflection and action were like some kind of recipe or instruction for making a thing, the thing of learning, or stimulus–response theory is used as if to suggest that certain repeated procedures will lead to a thing called 'learning' being somehow lodged in the mind or brain. Now it may be that when we learn things, chemicals and so on *do* get lodged in areas of the brain, and this may be a very important fact for the psychologist in Fieldnote 2. It may even be very important for the advancement of medical understanding and treatment of disease, but to say that this is what learning *is*, would be an odd use of language, not because learning is not that particular thing, but because it is no sort of a thing.

When we speak of learning, we are speaking not of a thing but of a set of relationships involving change and a conscious subject (except in the metaphorical sense in which computers may be said to learn). The nature of those relationships depends on our theory at one level (for example, competing theories concerning the ways in which social positioning influences learning), but the issues that are brought into this relationship depend on our theory at a different level: whether we are, for example, considering learning as psychologists, sociologists, philosophers, and so on.

From this it would seem that my colleagues in Fieldnote 2 were sharing their theories at the second level – as sociologist, philosopher, and so on – but had not yet entered into any debate at the first level. This might come later when they go on to consider, for example, whether they learn better when they are given a wide degree of autonomy in choosing their activity, or whether they require their activity to be structured for them by someone who knows more about the subject matter.

This is, of course, an over-simplification, for as soon as one uses the term 'better' in relation to learning, one is presupposing some kind of criteria for what constitutes being 'better'. This is the question that those who speak of 'effective learning' so often avoid. What is it effective for? For knowing the truth about the world; for being able to get a more satisfying job; for being able to be a more moral person, or help create a more just society? All such questions involve values and yet further questions (about, say, justice or truth) and are therefore political.

In a comprehensive review of the literature in higher education teaching and learning (Entwistle 1992), barely a reference is made to the fact that any discussion of learning must involve a consideration of values. The subject is treated as though we all know what learning is (even if it is difficult to measure it or teach) and what it is for, and that the only problem we have is how best to do it. Indeed, in the following extract, as part of a discussion of 'student-centred learning', Entwistle seems to deny that choices of teaching methods involve questions of value concerning power relationships.

> However, it is not difficult to imagine why some teachers become uneasy about these methods [student-centred learning] when they are so explicitly linked by some commentators to radical changes in power relationships within education. Those links are, however, *by no means an essential* component either in justifying the importance of personal engagement in learning or in accepting that education is essentially a social process.
>
> (Entwistle 1992: 10, my emphasis)

Now while these 'commentators' to whom Entwistle is referring may have got wrong the relationship between student-centred learning and power relationships, to say that we can consider student-centred learning without reference to power relationships is to miss the *educational* significance of what is being discussed. To maintain that education is somehow politically neutral, and just about methods that can be applied in the service of any political ideology, seems to me to be particularly naïve and potentially dangerous.

From the perspective of the enquiring university teacher, such a viewpoint is not *educational*, for an *educational* discussion must transcend both of the levels of theory outlined above. It is not about merely the best method, nor about adopting a particular disciplinary perspective. It must inevitably concern itself with questions of value.

Looked at from this perspective, the discussion between my colleagues reported in Fieldnote 2 was not yet *educational* in this sense. They were not confronting the value positions implicit in their outlines of what they thought was important. They were, however, speaking from frameworks for understanding that were very important to them. The microbiologist who spoke of synapses, for example, actually cares about these things. The disciplinary basis of his work is an expression of his values; it plays an important part in his identity. The absent philosopher might have wanted to know what it all means, and I take this to be not merely an intellectual game (in the trivial sense), but something that really matters to her *as a philosopher*. It is not difficult to see how discussion about the values and purposes of education might come out of the kind of exchange reported above.

For example, the psychoanalyst might express the view that the purpose of learning is for the individual to develop by coming to terms with, or gaining some control over, patterns of behaviour formed in early childhood. The sociologist may then express the different view that the purpose of learning is to transform social relationships. These two accounts of the purposes of education express values that may well be in conflict. Working within such an area of potential conflict is a fundamental aspect of *educational* discussion. It is one that enables critiques of different disciplinary perspectives (or 'underlying theories') to emerge.

I am making an assumption here, which is that what the lecturers who participate on the course do and say about what they do actually matter to them, and are an expression of their values, even if they may not be able to articulate those clearly. It is an assumption that must underpin any attempt to invite students to reflect seriously upon whatever is in front of them. It underpins a range of perspectives, from Carl Rogers, with the importance he attaches to 'genuineness' (Rogers 1978) to Habermas (1972) and his view that by the very act of engaging in language we are assenting to a democratic principle, which, among other things, assumes that we take each other's contribution to discourse seriously (or at least, try to create the conditions in which we can do this). As a theoretical assumption, it also underpins the broad field of humanistic social psychology (Harré and Secord 1972).

I hope now to have identified three important principles that under-pinned the course described in Chapter 3, and that can provide a basis for the university teacher's enquiry. These are that the work draws upon the *diverse disciplinary commitments* that people bring to their enquiry; that it acknowledges that educational practice is *value laden*; and that, in its process, it assumes that *participants should be taken seriously* and be open to exploring their values as well as their knowledge in order to develop their educational understanding and practice.

I now want to indicate a model for understanding the process of a course that has the aim of improving learning through the teacher's sustained enquiry. It is a model that gives expression to the above principles in the context of a group of people interacting with one another. It is suggestive of an 'underlying theory', or rather a heuristic device, for conceptualizing an educational process.

This model conceives of the course as drawing upon three contexts of knowledge, each of which have a critical influence upon the others, and which together constitute the curriculum of the course. The role of the course tutor is to attempt to engage knowledge derived from these three contexts into a critical relationship.

Contexts of knowledge

Fieldnote 3

As the session above (Fieldnote 2) continued, an interesting discussion of the different perspectives developed, but later the conversation turned towards considering a particular problem that one of the participants wanted to address in his teaching. This concerned how he should intervene in tutorials in order to encourage one particular female student to contribute. The student always seemed to be silent and the teacher found that whatever he did, this student seemed to remain uninvolved in the discussion. This led to the group sharing instances that they had all experienced of this problem in different contexts.

While this sharing of stories appeared to have some value, we didn't get far in solving the problem. I wondered whether the earlier discussion about what learning was could help us here. Comments were made by the microbiologist that his idea about learning couldn't really help, because there was no way we could get inside the student's brain to find out what – if anything – was happening! The sociologist, however, wondered whether perhaps the student lacked confidence. Perhaps this was something to do with the fact that she was the only female in a male group. Or was she from an ethnic minority group, he wondered. The psychotherapist didn't say much, although I wondered what he had in mind when he suggested that it might be helpful to talk to the student on her own some time to find out how she felt. During much of this part of the discussion, the sociologist continued to develop his idea that the silent student's problem might be due to gender or ethnic considerations.

Then a woman participant, who had been silent for much of the session, intervened to say that she felt that the sociologist was dominating the discussion. Although her voice was quiet, I felt that she was really very angry. She said the sociologist had done most of the talking. Her disclosure seemed particularly ironic since the gist of his comments had been largely about how women are often intimidated by men in conversation! Someone else in the group, however, felt that the sociologist's ideas were really interesting and that anyone was free to intervene if they wanted to. This led to rather a difficult conversation in which I invited anyone to comment on how free they felt to contribute to our discussions. One person stayed silent on this issue.

Communication is a process of exchange. In this fieldnote we can see how the discussion develops through three distinct phases: the first a discussion of the ideas about learning; the second a sharing of experience about a particular problem; and the third an attempt to address the group's own process of interaction.

Each of these kinds of exchange draws upon a different context of knowledge. The knowledge claimed by the participants in Fieldnote 2 and developed at the start of Fieldnote 3 about 'What is learning?' relates to *public contexts*. Such knowledge derives from public texts, which may or may not be from the participant's own disciplinary field. The criteria for the validity of claims to this kind of knowledge are, in principle, public and draw upon canons established within the discipline. While such canons may be in dispute, such disputation is public, or can be made public. When participants share, or contest, knowledge of this sort, some are likely to be viewed as more knowledgeable than others. The knowledge to which they refer, however, is in principle accessible to anyone in the group through public texts. The final arbiter to knowledge claims of this sort is *reason*. As the conversation developed at the beginning of Fieldnote 3, each participant might have drawn upon further theories and insights from their discipline to elaborate their claim about the nature of learning. In fact, they never reached agreement because, in an important sense, they were each addressing a rather different question, but they could at least have drawn upon evidence from the public domain to support their claims.

In the later part of the meeting, when the participants were discussing the problem of the silent student and sharing instances of similar problems, the discussion referred directly to personal and professional experience. This second context, the *personal context* is, in principle, private. Here the individual participants were authorities on what was, after all, their own personal experience. The 'texts' they were drawing on were not public texts; rather they were the private recollections or 'stories' that each constructed in order to give meaning to their experience. When participants shared this kind of knowledge they may have become aware of their differences and, as a result, changed their point of view. At the end of the day, however, the sense they made of their own experience cannot be challenged by anyone else's experience. Since their own experience was peculiar to them alone, they were inevitably the final judges of the knowledge that derived from it.

In the third part of the conversation, when they were discussing the woman's feeling that she was being dominated, and the group's process, the conversation was drawing upon the third source of knowledge: the *shared context*. The 'text' in question here was the process of the group's work. This text – the process of interaction itself – was, of course, open to very different interpretations. What one person experienced as a dominating man, who wouldn't let her get a word in edgeways, another experienced as an interesting and knowledgeable expert, whose contribution was valued. The events to which it related, however, were ones in which each member participated. In one respect, this shared context is even more public for the participants than the public context, since they each have an equal access to it.

Any sharing or disputing of knowledge from the shared context can always be related back to the shared experience. For example, on this occasion, the woman who felt dominated referred to the length of time the man spent on his speeches. This observation could have been challenged by others in the group. It is the only context that has a shared reference. In another respect, however, it is even more personal than the personal context, for the way in which any individual responds to the process, interprets it or feels about it, may often be intensely personal and revealing of their feelings and identity. Here, the woman who felt dominated might have felt very vulnerable in raising the matter because, she may have felt, it exposed her own weakness. It was, perhaps, only later that these feelings of vulnerability were transformed into anger, which I sensed when she spoke up. Another participant, who remained silent on this issue, may have been silent because he was reluctant to get involved in what he saw as a personal criticism. In an interchange of this sort, the most important criteria for effective communication is *openness*.

There are no hard and fast boundaries between these contexts. One can easily merge into the other, and each interacts significantly with the other. They do, however, work as a conceptual device for analysing a communicative process. They can also be used in the analysis of a whole curriculum, that is, on the complete series of sessions, reflections and other events that make up a course.

For example, a traditional academic course of lectures would normally highlight the public context. The curriculum would be seen in terms of the public knowledge defined by the syllabus and validated by reason. Here, a student who draws upon the shared context to say, for example, how they feel about being lectured at, would be viewed as behaving inappropriately, unless, of course, such behaviour was understood and legitimated in terms of 'student feedback', which is normally given when, and only when, it is requested.

A course that makes use of 'active learning' methods might also draw upon the personal context of experience in order to give meaning to knowledge derived from the public context. A sociology tutorial in which students are invited to draw upon their personal experience in order to assess, for example, some theory of social class, would be engaging in the personal context. Any continuing professional development course is likely to involve at least some reference to the personal context in which people test their own experience against ideas from the public domain.

Participants in a group therapy session, on the other hand, are likely to highlight the shared context, emphasizing their feelings about the process they are engaged in, and relating this to knowledge derived from the personal context. They are unlikely to dwell upon the public context of knowledge; to do so would be seen as 'intellectualizing'.

Lovers under the full moon are likely to dwell exclusively within the shared context. To start talking here about one's personal context of past experience, or one's knowledge of the latest developments in the psychology of sex, could lead to an abrupt ending of the relationship!

I want to suggest that an important feature of an educational course in which university teachers enquire into their practice is that it should draw upon all three contexts, because each exercises a critical influence upon the other.

Towards critical interdisciplinarity

Referring back to Fieldnote 2, when the lecturers were sharing their ideas about learning a significant question for them to go on to consider was how their understanding of the nature of learning (from their disciplinary standpoint) relates to their practice as teachers and learners. They might also want to draw upon educational texts within the public context in order to help them to see the relationships between disciplinary knowledge and educational practice. However, the basis of their values, their sense of their own expertise and their identity, are likely to derive largely from their disciplinary field. It may thus be this disciplinary context, rather than their limited knowledge of the field of education, that would provide the basis for their educational understanding. The *differences* between their disciplinary contexts would then stimulate critique in relation to these ideas. This becomes clear in Fieldnote 4, relating to a group two years later who were also considering the question of assessment.

Fieldnote 4
The group had decided that this session should start with one of
them, a cell biologist, giving a brief presentation of his ideas about
feedback. In this, he drew attention to the idea of feedback in cell
biology. If I understood him correctly, he appeared to be saying that
cells receive feedback from their environment, and that this is a mech-
anism by which they adapt to it so that they can continue to grow. He
suggested this as a metaphor for feedback to students. Perhaps the
purpose of us giving students feedback is that they can develop and
thrive.

Also in the group was a participant from the Department of Control
Engineering. In the discussion that followed, he said that in mechanical controlled systems, the purpose of feedback is to keep the performance of the system within predefined limits. If we took this as a
metaphor for feedback to students, then feedback would be a means
by which they are controlled, rather than a means by which they grow.

I thought that these metaphors could also be applied to thinking
about feedback from students to lecturers about their teaching. Is it a
means by which teachers grow and thrive in their professional practice, or is it a means by which they are controlled? But I didn't share
these thoughts with the group at the time.

In this fieldnote we can see how different disciplines can contribute a
rich source of metaphors for helping us to think about our teaching, but
the aim is to develop educational practice, not just ideas. If discussion is
restricted to the public context, then there is no assurance that the knowledge derived will be transferred to professional practice. The cell biologist
and the control engineer in Fieldnote 4 need to explore these ideas within
their own practice as teachers, which is the personal context of their knowledge. Which of these metaphors, theories or stories about feedback are
most valuable to them as educators?

This two-way interaction between the personal context of practice, and
the public context of theory makes possible the development of new practices and more developed theories. The broad field of action research (see,
for example, Carr and Kemmis 1986), with its roots in critical theory, is
based on this idea.

However, interaction between the personal and public contexts is not
enough. There also needs to be an appropriate *shared context* for critical
debate to take place. Action researchers draw upon Habermas's concept of
an 'ideal speech community' (Habermas 1974) as one in which 'symmet-
rical communication' (Grundy and Kemmis 1984: 16) can take place, undistorted by the influence of power. In real social situations such as courses,
however, power always has a distorting influence over reason. By addressing
the *shared context*, participants can begin to address these distortions and

create a speech community that is a little closer to the ideal for critical debate.

Reflection upon practice within the context of the available theoretical resources from the different disciplinary frameworks may lead to new insights, but unless one tests out such insights within the shared context itself, one is inevitably thrown back upon one's own personal resources as interpreter of one's practice. Opportunities for critique are then no longer available.

In Fieldnote 4 some ideas emerged about feedback that they later related to their work with their students, but once they used these insights to interpret the activity within the shared context of our present work together on the course, these ideas took on a sharper and more immediate reality. The opportunity for this arose several sessions after this last session.

Fieldnote 5
(Several meetings later.) The group were discussing how they would be presenting their portfolios for assessment. I felt somewhat awkward in this discussion, because it seemed to force me back into a tutorly role, rather than one of an equal collaborator in the enquiry. I suspect some of them felt the same. They wanted me to say something about how I would asses their work. I said that, as with the last module, I would read it and give them each a page or two of my comments, which could then be the subject of personal tutorials with them later.

I then reminded them of the conversation we had had several meetings ago when they talked about feedback as a means of promoting growth, or as a means of control. I asked whether they felt that my feedback to them on the portfolios would be viewed as a form of control or of growth. This led to a valuable discussion, which also served to deal with some of the tensions which I – and I believe they – felt about my assessing their work. It also led to several references about how it must feel to be a student being assessed.

This discussion of feedback took on an intense significance when directed at the group's work together. They transformed the group experience from being one in which the worlds of professional life and public knowledge were reflected upon, into one that reflects upon itself. In this way, the process of the course became the subject of its reflection. Critique now took on a different meaning. The question of student feedback having been enriched by different disciplinary insights, and developed by relating it to 'practice', was now subjected to the most rigorous critique of immediate experience.

To summarize, the heuristic model I have described is one in which the participants draw upon the full resources of knowledge within the group. These resources come not only from the variety of disciplinary perspectives offered by the participants, but also from their separate professional and personal experiences, and, most importantly, from their shared reflection upon the group's process itself. But this raises the question of the roles of the tutor and participants in this process. Who has responsibility for seeing that this happens, and how is it exercised? How does an academic become a student again and what is the experience like for them and for their tutor? These are the questions I shall turn to in Chapter 5.

Conclusion

Finally, to return to the original question concerning the underlying theory for a course aimed at developing university teaching, I have resisted the temptation to see *educational theory* as providing an overarching account of how educational thinking might develop on a course such as this. There is a wide literature in the field that may be described as *education*, and much of this has been of great value to course participants. Whether this literature comprises a discipline as such is debatable, however. Certainly the ideas I have used here draw upon understandings from psychology, sociology, philosophy, psychotherapy, and more, but to search for one specifically *educational* theory to draw together these diverse ways of thinking would seem to be an unnecessary as well as hopeless task. Perhaps the claim I am making for a course that aims to develop the teacher's enquiry into teaching is similar to the claim Lyotard made when he commented on a course designed to train teachers in philosophy:

> I have to confess to you that in my opinion educating and instructing aren't any more or less philosophical acts than banqueting or fitting out a ship. Philosophy is not a discrete terrain in the geography of the disciplines . . . You cannot be a master and master this course. You cannot open up a question without leaving yourself open to it. You cannot scrutinize a 'subject' (training, for example) without being scrutinized by it. You cannot do any of these things without renewing ties with the season of childhood, the season of the mind's possibilities.
>
> (Lyotard 1986: 115–16)

During a final course evaluation, one group of participants were invited to list the successes and failures of the course. As a success, they almost all agreed with one person's comment that the work had had a profound impact upon their ability to articulate educational questions and to relate these to the wider society, *and* had significantly changed their practice of teaching. An uncertainty that remained for them, however, was that they also nearly all agreed that, in spite of this success, they still did not feel they knew what educational theory was.

I am inclined to share their uncertainty.

5

Academic as Student

Introduction

It is exciting to engage with people who have different ideas and ways of looking at the world. Academic life has been portrayed as 'tribal' with different assumptions and cultural values being associated with different disciplines (Becher 1989). The way universities are organized tends to reinforce this and promote the stereotypes associated with these tribes. However, when the opportunity is provided to enquire into university teaching with others, such stereotypes are readily challenged as people gain a raised awareness of the assumptions associated with teaching in their own discipline, and begin to question these and learn from others.

In Chapter 4 a model was suggested for working together in a way that enables this kind of critical challenge to emerge with the result that teaching is developed. This model can be summarized in terms of the resources that collaborative enquiries can draw upon (Fig. 5.1).

Figure 5.1 Resources for learning

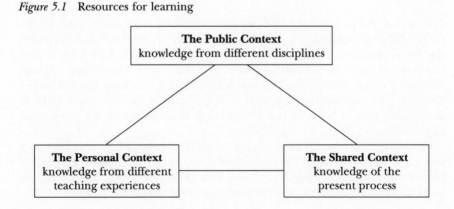

The advantage of conducting enquiries collaboratively is that it makes it possible to draw upon a wide range of knowledge from these different perspectives. This range, however, is not necessarily available to the group. For example, a course that concentrated on presentations from the field of knowledge of the tutor alone, would not enable this to happen. Nor would it happen on a course that only concentrated on sharing the participants' experiences of teaching.

The problem, then, is how are a group of people to work together in a way that realizes the potential of what each can bring from their different backgrounds? No predetermined list of outcomes can assure that this potential will be realized, because it depends on what the participants each bring to the collaborative work. The cell biologist and the control engineer of Fieldnote 4 both gained insights that were to have an effect on their approach to assessing students, but these insights were a consequence of these particular people collaborating and bringing the metaphors from their own discipline to bear upon the issue. They are not outcomes that could have been predicted in advance.

Since the work of the enquiring teacher is a form of research, its outcomes cannot be known in advance. Research that knew its outcome before it started wouldn't be research. All we can ever do is maximize the chances for valuable learning and discoveries to take place. In order to do this here, a process is required in which participants contribute from their own experience and knowledge from all three contexts.

In this chapter I want to consider how such a process is developed. What is the role of a tutor or facilitator? How is it experienced by the participants? To what extent is negotiation possible? These questions inevitably raise a number of dilemmas that must be faced if we want to take collaborative enquiry seriously. In order to explore these questions I shall make use of fieldnote extracts relating to a range of activities aimed at developing teaching.

Deep and surface negotiation

The terms 'deep' learning and 'surface' learning have been used to describe different approaches to student learning, or different student learning styles (see, for example, Marton *et al.* 1993, 1997). The idea is that when we struggle with an idea, relate it to our other knowledge, explore its implications, and so on, this will lead to deep learning. On the other hand, a piece of information that is learnt parrot fashion leads only to surface learning. I want to use this metaphor of depth in the context of negotiation.

Fieldnote 6 introduces the concept of surface negotiation. It relates to a visit to a university Staff Development Unit by a well known expert on higher education teaching. I shall call him Professor Jones. The event was to be a two-hour seminar on developing student-centred learning.

Fieldnote 6

After introductions from the Director of Staff Development, Professor Jones approached the overhead projector and illuminated his first transparency outlining the programme for the day's meeting.

Twenty of us (academic staff) faced him in a formal layout of chairs and tables. His dark suit added to the air of formality, which I already felt to be somewhat at odds with the subject of student-centred learning. I had always thought this emphasized a more informal approach. Perhaps Professor Jones was also aware of this too, for he moved around uncomfortably, tried sitting on first one, then the other, of the tables in the front, removed his jacket, loosened his tie and made an 'ice-breaking' joke, which I cannot recall. He explained how half the time would be spent on him giving a presentation and the other half, after a short break, on questions and discussion.

At the end of this introduction, he moved away from the overhead projector, stepped forward a little and said: 'Now is that alright? Is that a reasonable plan for the morning?'

I don't know whether he expected anybody to raise any objection at this point, but no one did. There was just a somewhat embarrassed silence and then a few people mumbled something, which was taken to be an agreement.

This is a clear enough example of surface negotiation. Nothing is really negotiated. An agreement is sought by Professor Jones, and no one withholds their consent, but we do not really know how people felt about his plan for the seminar. They were free to object or make a different suggestion, because they were asked, but the context of a formal meeting signified by the arrangement of furniture, the clothing of the visiting speaker, and his obviously well prepared plan, made it difficult to consider an alternative. Even more significantly, the purpose of the event would have been seen in terms of providing an opportunity to listen to an expert. What value his expertise if we do not even go along with his plan?

Nevertheless, Professor Jones, an expert on student-centred learning, probably realized that negotiation is an important part of providing a context for learning. He would quite probably have liked to work with us in a way that was negotiated in a student-centred fashion but, like us participants, felt that this was not the context for it.

Using the idea of the 'shared context' of knowledge developed in Chapter 4, we can see that Professor Jones, by inviting us to assess his plan for the seminar, is apparently attempting to move the conversation into the shared context. This is emphasized by his body language too, in stepping forward towards the participants. Any response to his question is a comment on the present 'here-and-now' process. The fact that the participants did not respond to his question, or only did so with embarrassment, is not surprising.

People do find it difficult to address the immediate shared context and, in this case, any alternative to agreement could be understood as something of a personal challenge to him.

Clearly, a negotiative stance like this one, with little expectation of real discussion of how work is to proceed, is not going to lead to collaboration among the group. I do not raise this in order to decry the value of such a seminar. It was, in fact, quite interesting; and collaboration was not the intention here. Rather, I want to suggest that the kind of negotiation required for our model to work would mean much more than merely seeking consent.

At the other extreme to surface negotiation such as this, is deep negotiation. In the example of this that follows, we can see how such negotiation moves the conversation into the shared context as people start to respond to their experience of each other. This illustration is drawn from a week long residential course, which had aims similar to those described in the preceding chapters, but was run for teachers who had a role as teaching consultants or mentors within their subject area. As tutor, I had in mind that the detailed agenda for our work would arise from the group concerning the problems they expect to meet in their departments as mentors. Soon after beginning the course, I prepared the ground for this negotiation by initiating the following 'workshop' activity.

Fieldnote 7

There were ten of us in the group. Sitting in a circle, I suggested that we give an hour to this activity. At the end of the hour, we could continue if we felt that would be useful. I described what I had in mind.

The aim was to devise a set of ground rules which would operate during the course. To do this, any participant would suggest a ground rule, which could be debated. If all the participants agreed with this rule, it would then be written on a large piece of paper and placed on the floor in the middle of the group. Once a rule was on the floor, everyone had to obey it. They also had the right – indeed the obligation – to challenge anyone they felt was infringing it. If, at any time, anyone wished to oppose a rule (which they must have agreed to earlier) then the rule was withdrawn or amended in some way until everyone agreed with it again. Any ground rule must have the assent of all the group.

After a few questions in which the rules of this 'game' were checked out, everyone agreed to give it a go.

I was determined to say little once it had started.

Soon John suggested a rule that no one should interrupt while someone else was speaking. Sarah said that this was unnatural: people don't really converse without interruption. This point seemed to be resolved after a little discussion, with everyone agreeing that this kind of course was not really 'natural' anyway, and that the rule might help us to listen to one another. John then asked if everyone agreed to the rule. There were nods around the room and so he wrote it down and put it on the floor.

The question of listening to one another was pursued further. How could we make a rule that everyone must listen to what is said? Andy commented that you could not check up that the rule was being obeyed, so you couldn't challenge someone over it, so it wouldn't be a good rule. Rules had to concern observable behaviour.

Further discussion about this began to get more heated, with John, supported by Jane, arguing for clear-cut formal rules, while Sarah protested that such rules were ridiculous if we were really going to talk to one another.

Attempting to sum things up so far, Mike said: 'Now where have we got to so far? We've decided that we should always listen to everyone . . .'

'Who's this "we" you're talking about?', interrupted Sarah, angrily. 'Are you saying I've agreed to this? You speak for yourself and let me speak for myself.'

The temperature rose as Jane challenged Sarah for interrupting, then Sarah returned to deal with Mike.

The conversation over the next half hour was at times intense, but there were pauses while people gathered their thoughts, or even exchanged the occasional smile. Resulting from the argument between Sarah and Mike, which by now had become more friendly, it was agreed that there should be a rule that entitled people only to speak on their own behalf. After several attempts were made to put this into words for a 'rule', a form was finally settled upon along the lines of: 'People must own their own statements and speak for themselves using 'I' rather than 'we'.

By the time the hour was up, everyone was listening to one another intensely. There seemed to be a sensitivity that was not so much the product of us obeying the rules, but the result of the process of working towards them.

The group felt that the activity was valuable and that we should continue with it in the next session since it had direct relevance to how we interact with colleagues and clients, as well as helping us towards a better way of communicating on the course.

This meeting set out with the task of working towards a contract or set of ground rules that would be agreed to by all the group. The idea of a 'learning contract' has been developed in several institutions, particularly on courses for more mature students (see, for example, Stephenson and Laycock 1993). It has also been said that an adult way of learning is best established when a group agrees to and respects and values each other, and that this is best achieved through a contract that establishes ground rules (Egan 1974).

Much less has been said about how such a contract might be achieved. The assumption is often that the teacher sets out the ground rules and persuades the students to agree. This is what I wanted to avoid on this occasion. Real ownership of the rules would only be achieved, I felt, if the participants played a democratic role in devising the rules.

In the process of doing this, however, what was to emerge was not so much a set of rules as a raised awareness. It was the negotiative process itself that raised this awareness, rather than the product – the set of rules. Of significance here in terms of our model of the contexts of knowledge, is that this process involved people in reflecting upon the process itself, thereby drawing upon the 'shared context'. The 'game' or workshop placed everyone in a situation in which they had to give each other feedback on how they felt about each other's contribution. At times this led to an uncomfortable intensity, but as these confrontations were worked through, so the individuals gained trust in each other.

In fact, this workshop did continue further and, without doubt, led to an environment in which people were prepared to contribute from their own knowledge and experience, were able to challenge each other within a context of mutual support, and were thus able to move between the different contexts of knowledge.

In this case my suggestion of the workshop was a powerful intervention. Having decided to join in the game, my contributions as tutor were inevitably given special value. I sought to avoid this here by being 'determined to say little once it had started'. But such silence does not serve to diminish my power. Indeed, the silence of the tutor (or the head of department at a staff meeting, for that matter) often reinforces power rather than reduces it. Thus, in this case, although my workshop did move the group into a way of working in which they were able to share their thoughts and feelings openly, it also, in the longer term, created a dependency upon myself as facilitator of this process. This is fine for a short course, but if the aim is to develop a group of people who are to work together as colleagues in projects of collaborative research that will continue without the permanent facilitation of a tutor, it can lead to too much dependence upon the tutor's presence.

The problem here cannot be avoided. Any attempt to establish ground rules requires some further ground rules to be accepted to guide this attempt. But these second order ground rules would themselves have to be established with recourse to some third order ground rules, and so on, *ad infinitum*. This is the diplomatic problem of 'talks' between groups of people in dispute often being preceded by 'talks about talks', and even these are sometimes preceded by more preliminary 'talks about talks about talks'. This is why negotiation between parties in dispute is always difficult to get going.

The same dilemma arises for any teacher who is trying to negotiate a new way of interacting with students different from their current expectations. As soon as the teacher introduces the innovation, they increase their own power by becoming the 'expert' of this innovatory process. This is a particular problem for any tutor or facilitator who attempts to move a group into a climate of open negotiation, which is required if they are to work according to our model.

Deception and manipulation occur when an appearance of negotiation is offered merely to seduce the participants into a sense of ownership of a process, without actually empowering them to make strategic decisions. However, even such manipulation is paradoxical, as Fieldnote 8 illustrates. This concerns Nigel, a fairly experienced lecturer from a medical science department. We were meeting to discuss his portfolio of writings submitted for assessment after the second term's work on the Masters course described in Chapter 3.

Fieldnote 8

In Nigel's portfolio he had written about how he felt the course had been what he called 'a conversion experience'. He obviously felt good about this. He was happy to be 'converted' from what he now sees as a traditional university teacher into someone who he now feels is much more sensitive to the processes of learning. He goes on to explain how this was achieved through a process that was often difficult. It involved painstaking negotiations and often periods of silence in the group as people struggled with what they wanted to say. The dénouement of his piece of writing, however, was his view that this change had only occurred because he had been manipulated. Had he really been free to choose the kind of course he went on, he would have chosen something much more conventional. His conclusion to this evaluative piece of writing was therefore that he had been manipulated, and he was glad that he had been.

While appreciating Nigel's openness about this, I was uneasy when we met to talk about it at our next supervision. When I confronted him with the issue of his feeling that I had manipulated him, he confirmed that he did feel that way, and that he was glad that I had. We talked about this paradoxical realization. There seemed to be something odd in the idea of being glad to have been manipulated. I think the conclusion he drew from the discussion was that perhaps all 'conversion' experiences are ones in which one is manipulated. He felt that the changes that this course demanded required such a conversion for him.

I still felt uneasy about this idea of being a manipulator.

By describing the process he had been through as one of 'manipulation' Nigel was, perhaps, using language a little provocatively. In no sense was he criticizing me, but rather highlighting the somewhat paradoxical idea that certain kinds of learning almost inevitably involve an element of manipulation. The issue here is a general one for anyone who wants to promote forms of learning that are broadly 'student-centred'. It is commonly believed that the transition from 'teacher-centred' to 'student-centred' ways of working – whether with undergraduates or professional adults as students – represents a shift in power from the teacher to the student. To some extent this is the case, but the very attempt to make this shift by 'facilitating' the change is itself an exercise of power. The power I exercised over Nigel was the result not of my overtly imposing my agenda upon him, but of my knowingly facilitating a process that was intended to move him from being a 'traditional' teacher towards becoming a more 'student-centred' one.

Often, when I have worked with colleagues on this kind of course, participants have commented that they view me as an equal in the group. Although such comments may be made in all honesty, it is often a naïve view, for the power of the tutor resides not so much in their teaching method – whether directive or facilitative – but in the *fact* of their being the tutor. The social relationships of power that exist between students and teachers cannot simply be removed by facilitative devices. Indeed, more covert or subtle forms of facilitation can represent a stronger exercise of power than the overt exercise of power through didactic methods. This was Nigel's realization here. Only when writing up his portfolio and reflecting upon the events of the term's work, did he understand the extent to which I had been facilitating the group with a particular aim in mind. And, moreover, my aim had been one to which, at the outset, he would not have agreed.

This indeed presented me with a dilemma. On the one hand I value openness and explicitness, and these qualities of interaction are prerequisites for the model I have proposed. On the other hand, it was my *lack* (deliberate or otherwise) of explicitness in the way I facilitated the process of the group that Nigel considered led to his 'conversion' towards a view that was more sensitive to the processes of learning.

In order for the model I have proposed to work, participants need to be able to address the group process in order to draw upon the shared context. Communication about the shared context – perceptions about what is happening at present – is necessary in order to evaluate and improve the learning process. It also enables us to learn from this in ways that can then be applied to other teaching contexts, as we saw in the Fieldnote 5 about assessment in Chapter 4.

The importance of individuals considering the process by which they collaborate is not peculiar to this kind of work, or even to teaching as a whole. Theories of management that focus on the idea of the 'Learning Company', emphasize this (Pedlar *et al.* 1988). It is difficult, however, for the facilitator or teacher or manager to be explicit about this for the reasons that Nigel, in Fieldnote 8, suggested. That is, had I been explicit, he felt he probably would have rejected – or perhaps failed to have understood – what I had in mind.

In the following extract from the portfolio of a course participant we can see how he experienced this problem as a manager. John is the Director of Sheffield Television. Although he had joined the Masters course on teaching and learning, he did not teach students, but directed a unit, which provided television support for staff. He understood, however, that his work was educational and that is why the course was valuable to him. Here he reflects on his difficulty with being explicit about the process of managing his unit in a collaborative manner.

> A problem I face is being explicit about what I am doing. I find it impossible to say, 'OK guys, we're all members of a collaborative group who can learn from one another, support one another, and one person's problems are all our problems . . .'. If I did say that I fear I would be faced with ten incredulous faces. When I've tried to explain our . . . process to colleagues, I sense a lack of comprehension. So I see the notion of group process as always being something that will remain largely unarticulated in the unit.
>
> . . . I have been told that some people find the tendency of mine to involve the group annoying ('leaders are paid to lead'). Not only that, consultation slows things down, which sometimes cuts across the need to respond quickly and decisively to situations and to ensure that the trains stay running on time.
>
> (Stratford 1999: 10)

John's difficulty is getting his staff to accept what might be called a more negotiative or 'person-centred' approach to working, which would involve them giving attention to their processes of interaction. Rogers calls such a transformation in practice a 'quiet revolution' (Rogers 1978: 29–140). Here John senses 'a lack of comprehension' when he attempts to introduce such an idea. His negotiative stance is also resisted because they want to 'ensure that the trains stay running on time'.

I have often heard university teachers complain that students resist the introduction of more negotiated ways of working because they cannot understand the point and they want to 'ensure that they learn the stuff for the exams on time'. How similar the problems of the manager and the teacher are in relation to developing a community of learners! As soon as the manager or teacher behaves in a way that is contrary to expectation, the students, or managed staff, are likely to meet this with incomprehension. Of course, the particular nature of student expectations will depend on the social norms and values of the culture. In Chapter 8 I explore the cultural significance of this, but in the present context there is a natural resistance – often expressed by embarrassment – to being open about how we are relating to one another in the 'shared context'. This can make it difficult to draw upon all the group's resources of knowledge.

Power is the root of the problem here. The model I have proposed requires that individuals have an equal power to draw on all of their resources, including their perceptions of the present process. The ability to realize this in practice, however, is always limited by the extent to which they are unable to eliminate the inequalitites in power relationships within the group. Where the group meet within the context of assessed coursework, the power of the tutor or teacher is particularly prominent. When the course relates to students who are also peers, colleagues and co-enquirers with the tutor running the course – as would often be the case in professional development courses on university teaching – this power relationship can seem particularly paradoxical.

In order to explore how this is experienced, I shall draw on an instance that arose among another group on the same Masters course. Here, however, the context was not a series of face-to-face meetings but a series of email interactions. The participants to this were a group of five who had been meeting over the past year with me as their tutor. During the previous month, unbeknown to me, they had decided that they would not submit a portfolio of writings on curriculum issues for assessment, as was the normal expectation. I became aware of this when I received the following email message from them.

Dear Stephen,

Bob, Robert, Robin, Ceri and Lin have decided to present a joint portfolio on curriculum issues (this decision being just such an issue). After considerable debate (copies of which will be delivered to you in the next hour) we have agreed that, as part of the group, you should not only know of our decision but also be invited and encouraged to participate in the portfolio (which we intend to carry out by email). We realise that this poses problems (do you want to be actively involved where you haven't before; what will be the effect on assessment? etc.) as you will see discussed but we feel that our decision to tell you is closely bound up in wanting you to participate. Please read through the arguments and then get back to us . . .

Robert, Ceri, Lin, Bob and Robin

Within the hour, I found, in my pigeon hole, a file containing 45 pages of their email correspondence, which had led to their decision to send me this message. Much of this email discussion concerned issues of power. In the following extract from an email message from Robin to the rest of the group, he outlines the issues as he saw them, and presented a case for not inviting me to join; a view that the group eventually rejected. It makes reference to earlier comments from another member of the group, Bob.

. . . If we now invite Stephen to participate in our joint work, how much will Stephen's role be unequal in the group portfolio, just as it is unequal in the group's discussions? . . .

[in an earlier email] Bob wrote: 'Stephen is different to us yes, in the group work we have considered how the gulf between tutor and student can be reduced. Stephen has introduced us to a curriculum that invites us to share control. I suggest that we now invite Stephen to share in the portfolio exercise.'

It may be possible to reduce the gulf, but the difference will still be there, with us and Stephen as with us and our students. To invite Stephen to share control is to cede control disproportionally [*sic*] . . .

Bob again: 'There is a question of risk in the exercise; to tell Stephen would reduce the risk in taking control of the curriculum; but do we have the right to take control?'

I would answer emphatically 'yes'. Any control we have is only that which Stephen has ceded to us. Our freedom in our first two portfolios was there because Stephen gave it to us. The format could have been more constricting, but it wasn't. Any freedom we have to act now is solely courtesy of Stephen. We have already taken control to the extent that we have decided to construct a joint portfolio. Involving Stephen is simply to return some power and control to the tutor and away from the student.

I do not believe we should be involving Stephen, for the above reasons and also because it places the assessment status of the portfolio in an uncharted area. If our submission of a joint portfolio presents difficulties for Stephen in assessment terms, how much more would that be true of a portfolio in which he has participated. This is largely an issue for Stephen, but one which we should take account of in planning our course of action.

Bob once more: 'The group have always advocated negotiated curricula but where is the negotiation? Do students have absolute rights to set the agenda? Are we not now abusing our power as students, as we may have previously abused our power as tutors?'

I take the point that negotiation of the curriculum does perhaps require us to discuss our proposed format with Stephen. But I do not think Stephen should be involved in the content of the portfolio beyond that.

I suggest a middle way. We tell Stephen what we plan, that we are already embarked down that course, but that we wish to involve him in some way in the process. We could ask that he provide a piece of writing for inclusion in the portfolio on the tutor's perspective in this, which we can then discuss and comment on. We might for instance discuss with him how this form of portfolio could reinforce any feelings of a tutor-student divide that there may be in the group.

But for other topics and areas, I suggest that we should not involve Stephen. To have Stephen taking part in all the writings would to my mind make the exercise so safe that it would lose the edge which I hope would be its strength. In other words, it will become a 'namby pamby wishy washy vegetarian' sort of portfolio [a reference to an earlier comment]. If we're going to take control of our curriculum, let's do it properly with no half-measures.

Robin

The fact that these five students on a course took the initiative to over-turn the normal assessment requirement of individual portfolios, and to present their decision to me as a *fait accompli* indicates that they are consid-erably empowered, presumably to some extent at least as a result of the course experience so far. What Robin recognizes here, however, is that this empowerment does not lead to a denial of my power as the tutor: '*any freedom we have is solely courtesy of Stephen*'. I have that power as an inescapable consequence of being the tutor. What he presents is a view that although they can use their power to make the decision to write jointly, if I were involved, this would not be as an equal. Bob's argument is that the prin-ciple of negotiation should apply to them as well as to me. For them to pursue a course of action without any negotiation from me would, he feels, be to abuse his power as a student just as a tutor might abuse his power as a tutor.

Robin was eventually persuaded by the others that I should be invited to join in. I then decided to accept this invitation, negotiated with the external examiner concerning the innovation, and did take part in writings in a way that I judged enabled me finally to assess the contribution of each parti-cipant. This all involved much further negotiation. What remained clear, however, is that throughout this process I did not, and could not, have given up my power as the tutor. In the final analysis, the degree for which their work was to be assessed was a degree awarded by the university. Even if they were to assess their own contributions, such assessment would have to be moderated or agreed to by me as the representative of the institution. Self-assessment does not provide for a redistribution of power on course work any more than a department's self-assessment statement about the quality of its teaching redistributes power in national quality assurance pro-cedures. Self-assessment, like self-censorship, can be a means of even more effective centralized control.

Conclusion

In Chapter 4 I outlined a model for how a group of enquiring teachers might draw on all of their resources of knowledge in their collaborative work. In this chapter I have explored how the process of negotiation can enable this way of working to develop but, in the process, raises some rather paradoxical issues, which largely centre on the distribution of power. The main conclusion to emerge is that however 'empowering' the tutor's facilita-tion of the course might be, the tutor cannot step out of the position of power that is constructed by the role, even though the 'student' may be a university teacher of equal (or senior) status to the 'tutor'.

The theoretical resources that I alluded to at the beginning of Chapter 4 throw some light on this situation. Carl Rogers's ideas about learning have emphasized a 'person-centred' (or 'student-centred') approach. According to this, the knowledge of the individual learners is the principle resource, rather than the expertise of the teacher or facilitator (Rogers 1969, 1978). Furthermore, this approach underlines the learner's, rather than the teacher's, responsibility for learning. The model that I have proposed views the learning as arising from the three contexts that each of the participants can draw on. It therefore also emphasizes the learners' roles as they each contribute from their own knowledge.

Critical theory, however, is a perspective that highlights the ways in which rational communication is distorted by the effects of unequal distribution of power. From this perspective, a Rogerian approach cannot be emancipatory or empowering for the learner unless an 'ideal speech community' is created in which each is free to communicate sincerely and honestly, undistorted by the influences of power. The purpose of action research – of which the university teacher's enquiry is a kind – is to improve our practices (of teaching, in this case) in such a way as to bring us closer to what Habermas has called an 'ideal speech community' (Thompson and Held 1982: 116–33), in which reason can overcome the vested interests of power.

In this chapter I have indicated some of the problems and limitations in trying to construct such an 'ideal speech community', but an ideal is only an ideal. The French philosopher Michel Foucault has criticized Habermas – an exponent of critical theory – for being 'Utopian' in even thinking that there could be a state of communication that would be free of the coercive effects of power. While Foucault, like Habermas, is concerned to challenge the domination that often results from power, he does not see power as an evil in itself:

> The problem is rather to know how you are to avoid in these practices – where power cannot not play and where it is not evil in itself – the effects of domination which will make a child subject to the arbitrary and useless authority of a teacher, or put a student under the power of an abusively authoritarian professor.
>
> (Foucault 1984: 18)

Foucault goes on to explore how the avoidance of such domination requires an ethic of care for the self. He does not mean that we should be egoistic, or look after our own interests above others, but rather turn our gaze upon ourselves in order to recognize ourselves and the truths that are important to us (Foucault 1984: 5). To put this another way, if we are to avoid abusing the power that the role of teacher or facilitator gives us, we need to make contact with the values that are deeply within ourselves. This is a more personal, private and reflective process. Pursuing this tack, I next want to explore how writing might play a role in making contact with our values and uncovering the truths that are important to us as university teachers.

6

Writing to (Re)discover a Love of Learning

The problem

Enquiry is also a private and reflective process: an inward struggle as well as an outward one. Chapters 4 and 5 have centred on the outward aspect of attempting to develop an environment for learning that is relatively free from the distorting influences of power. Now I want to address the inward aspect and show how writing can help us discover and articulate the values that underlie our teaching. This suggests an approach to writing that goes beyond the constraints of what is often called 'academic writing'. In this chapter I shall discuss the form of such writing, and in Chapter 7 will provide an illustration from my own professional experience.

'I want to inspire in my students a love of their subject.' This was the final sentence of Peter's dissertation as part of a Masters degree course on university teaching and learning (Carrotte 1994). Peter was an experienced teacher of dental students. His dissertation reported an investigation of his attempts to teach in a way that gave the students much more responsibility for their learning. For me, this sentence stood as an epilogue to the rest of the dissertation. This had reported on the design of an innovative course, the students' evaluation of it, further changes he made, and so on. But somehow the 'love' referred to in this final sentence had not been explored in the dissertation itself. It was, it seemed, an implicit value, which provided the motivation for the whole enquiry, but a value that he was unable to address directly.

It is difficult to think of a more fundamental educational aim for anyone who teaches in a university than to imbue in one's students a love of the subject. It seems to express what is at the heart of the vocation of teaching. Yet the statement sounds oddly romantic and naïve, or even empty, in the present context of concern for the quality of teaching. How can we speak of 'love' or 'inspiration' in evaluations and investigations when teachers are merely 'human resources' to be managed, teaching is framed around such notions as 'competence', and 'skill' is the determining criteria for evaluating both the outcomes and the processes of learning? Do we want to *write* this love? Or can it only live in silence in this context?

The term 'love' here might seem to contrast wildly with 'love' in the context of the erotic. But it is interesting to juxtapose the two. Turning to the word in its erotic sense, to speak of eros in the context of learning relationships is doubly illegitimate, for not only does eros refuse to submit to a language of skill and technique, but introducing sexuality infringes the cultural taboos that protect learners and teachers from powerful forces that can so easily lead to an abuse of the trust between them. Sex, in the context of education, is a risky business.

'Pleasure', 'eros' and 'seduction' are valuable terms for analysing learning processes, according to one of the few writers (McWilliam 1996) who has taken the risk of using such language. Here I want to take a slightly different tack, however, and focus more directly upon the *language* we use when we reflect upon and write about learning. How are we to reclaim a language of love and rediscover our own love of learning? (It has become difficult even to ask the question in this way without sounding merely sentimental or anti-intellectual.)

Similar changes have taken place in the ways in which the erotic and the educational have been written about and therefore reflected upon and researched. Both have been undermined by the dominance of the same technicist and market orientated influences. Understanding these influences will help us to see what we are up against in trying to write about, and to think about, such things as love in the context of our work as university teachers.

Eros and education

The Lovers' Guide One and *The Lovers' Guide Two* are the titles of two from a growing range of videos that have, in the UK, cornered an expanding market for 'educational' material concerning sexual relationships. The title of a third – *Supervirility* – gives a clearer hint of the macho values of virtuoso performance and endurance that underlie these technical portrayals of sex. Their promoters have convinced legislative bodies that such material is educational rather than pornographic. It is difficult to imagine how sexual activity could be more explicitly represented than it is in these videos. Every bodily juxtaposition is revealed with technical precision. These are not clever actors, but the real thing, doing it live; not for voyeuristic viewing but for serious educational purposes. Or so they say. Captions prominently displayed in the videos underline the importance of safe sex; the viewer is informed that the lovers being filmed are couples in steady relationships; between the action sequences the camera returns to one or two sex counsellors or therapists (the experts) who introduce the interesting things you can try out to enrich your sex life. In these videos, sexual practice, and even sexual relationships, submit to the discourses of technique and expertise.

Sexual matters are also addressed in a strikingly graphic way in a growing range of popular magazines. I recall my daughter (15 years old at the time) reading to me from her magazine about the calorific value of oral sex and its implications for the figure conscious. Only a couple of decades ago, legislation would have been used to prevent such material from being so readily available. How are we to account for this apparent liberalization in the face of a social climate that has been marked by a rhetoric that emphasizes the need for a 'return to family values', that has been so ready to view the AIDS epidemic as providing evidence for the need to return to traditional mores, and that has been increasingly unsympathetic to those whose sexuality deviates from normal heterosexual stereotypes? Are we moving into a more open climate as regards sexual matters, or are we experiencing greater oppression and control? Is such public access to facts and to techniques a liberalizing or oppressive feature of our times?

The same question arises in relation to educational representation. In the field of teaching in higher education, the CVCP booklet *The Impact on Learning Outcomes in Higher Education*, reviews a range of literature (Entwistle 1992). Much of it is concerned with the techniques of making teaching more 'learner-centred', placing more control into the hands of the students, and encouraging more active involvement on their part. Such a perspective is widely valued (although largely not practised) in higher education. The evaluations that students make of their own learning, and of their tutors' teaching, through student feedback questionnaires, are seen as being all important. Techniques of student self-assessment, profiling in which the students play a determining role, and negotiated learning contracts, are part of this development. At the same time, Students' Charters might also be seen as attempts to give students, as consumers or clients, an influence over their own learning that would have seemed revolutionary a couple of decades ago.

On the other hand, higher education has come increasingly under centralized control during this period. Teaching and learning, like research, are continually surveyed through quality assurance mechanisms, and students learn under increased pressure and lack of funds. How, then, are we to square what appears to be a greater concern for the students' learning and rights on the one hand with a move towards greater centralization and control on the other? Are we moving towards a more open climate for learning or a more tightly controlled one? Are we now more, or less, able to speak of a love of learning? Where can we find educational writing that addresses this fundamental motive of the teacher? And in particular, as teachers who enquire into our teaching, are we more, or less, able to write *of*, and write *from* this love?

Foucault (1981), in his *History of Sexuality*, suggests a reason for this apparent contradiction. He rejects the idea that a greater openness since the Victorian period in the ways in which we speak of sexual matters indicates a liberalization. It is, on the contrary, the very articulation of sexual matters through a shared language that enables sexuality to be more readily subject to social control. His argument serves to warn us that language may not always be a means of liberating that of which it speaks, but also of controlling it.

If we were to apply his analysis to the *Lovers' Guide* videos, we should soon conclude that by identifying and articulating explicitly and visually the specific behaviours of intimate sexual relationships, these activities thereby enter into a public arena: they become officially recognized practices, can be categorized as legitimate or deviant, safe or risky, honest or dishonest, and so on. In this way, such videos are not a liberalizing influence that works counter to other more oppressive tendencies, but are indeed part of the very means by which sexuality is controlled.

The same kind of analysis suggests that our teaching may also be imprisoned by the language that describes it, and that moves that at first sight might seem to empower students, may actually have a contrary effect. For example, recent research (Johnson 1998) suggests that the opportunity – of rather requirement – for students to provide feedback on the lecturers' teaching in end of course questionnaires is viewed, by many students as well as their teachers, as a limitation to the kind of open dialogue that would give students a voice. Likewise, student self-assessment, once built into the bureaucratic functions of the educational institution, can also become a means by which their learning is surveyed by the institution, rather than a move towards student autonomy. Such developments become a means of control rather than emancipation when they require judgements about learning and teaching to be made in narrow technical terms.

The idea of student empowerment (or sexual liberation) harks back to an earlier period – often characterized in the 'Western world' as the 'progressive movement' of the 1960s – when student power and sexual freedom were underpinned by a value position that was broadly liberationist. When such writers as Holt (1965), Postman and Weingartner (1969), Illich (1970) and Freire (1972a) wrote of the importance of giving learners a greater say in their own learning (or Greer (1970) wrote about the woman's control of her own sexuality), they were not merely indicating new techniques for a 'better' education (or sex life). Their writing questioned the very purposes of education and sexuality, and in particular the power relationships upon which these were based. Such ideas were seen as being revolutionary not just because they were innovations, but because they were part of a radically different concept of society.

But now we are in the age of post- (feminism, modernism or whatever), there is no ideological battle left. Or so we are led to believe. No longer are such innovatory ideas as student empowerment or women's rights held together by an overarching theme – or 'metanarrative', to use the jargon of postmodernism – of socialist or liberation politics. That political ideology would appear to have run its course and been replaced by a market place in which values, like sexual preferences and consumer products, are to be freely bought and sold. Now it is merely a matter of choosing your own particular pleasures and 'learning styles', and developing the techniques to satisfy them, or earning the power to buy them.

Peter had more in mind than technique when he wrote of wanting to inspire in his students a love of their subject. He had been broadly satisfied with his attempts to research and to develop his practice of teaching, and his dissertation was indeed excellent in many ways; but he appeared to feel that his writing as a form of reflection upon his practice did not give adequate expression to the values of love and inspiration that underlie his image of himself as a teacher. These were things of which he was unable to speak, except in this ironic epilogue. While the study had sought to gain some critical purchase on processes of learning, his written reflections some-how failed to capture his fundamental value position. If part of the problem here is the constraint of technical and bureaucratic ways of talking, writing and thinking about learning, what is to be done?

Let us pursue the parallels with love in the erotic sense a little further. The erotic is special because it cannot be identified with precision in the way a rational market place demands. It is always immutable to measure-ment, always open to reinterpretation, potentially subversive. In this way the erotic and the pedagogic are similar. Indeed, McWilliam (1996: 315) goes further and views the erotic not just as a metaphor for pedagogical work but as a central aspect of pedagogical experience. While this 'erotics of pedagogy', as she calls it, 'must not conflate *erotics* with sexual explicitness', it has much to do with pleasure, seduction and delight.

In the opening pages of *Written on the Body*, Jeanette Winterson writes with great precision about the imprecise emotion of love. Could this extract, perhaps, be read as relating to intellectual or educational love – the erotics of pedagogy – rather than to sexual love, which would appear to be the theme of the book? How would this look as part of an enquiry into a student's, or teacher's, love of the subject?

> Love demands expression. It will not stay still, stay silent, be good, be modest, be seen and not heard, no. It will break out in tongues of praise, the high note that smashes the glass and spills the liquid. It is no conservationist love . . . It's the clichés that cause the trouble. A precise emotion seeks precise expression. If what I feel is not precise then should I call it love?
>
> (Winterson 1993: 1)

How, then, are we to develop and represent a love of learning and teach-ing? How are we to resist 'the clichés that cause the trouble', the explicit-ness that reduces the erotic to the trendy and learning to educational technology? How can we reflect upon the practice of, say, 'student-centred learning' in a way that captures its fundamentally subversive, unpredictable and, as it were, 'erotic' quality rather than representing it merely as a form of technical accomplishment? What will be the form of such writing about our teaching and learning experience? How might it figure in an enquiry about university teaching?

Resisting positive language

It will need to resist what might be termed 'positivist' assumptions about the nature of language. Positivism is a philosophical perspective that claims that statements about value can be reduced to statements of fact. Or, to put this another way, anything we might say about what *ought* to be done (such as to love thy neighbour) can be fully expressed in terms of what *is* (such as that loving neighbours makes people happy). Now such a way of talking might be appropriate for discussing technical experiments where questions of moral values do not arise. It is also a useful perspective for the market place, where all questions of value are expressed in terms of price. But to say that the value of, say, a painting can be expressed solely in terms of its price or any other facts about it, is to have an impoverished concept of value. As Oscar Wilde puts it in *Lady Windermere's Fan*, 'a man who knows the price of everything and the value of nothing' is a cynic who knows nothing about love. Love can't be priced. Peter wanted to inspire in his students a love of the subject, but he could not have documented this love in terms of observable facts. Furthermore, such love of the subject is a value in itself, not simply a means by which students might learn more effectively.

The central structure of positivism is that of propositional logic. According to this structure, meaning is attributed in terms of the truth/falsehood of propositions: a proposition is held to be meaningful only if it can be conceived of as either true or false, otherwise it is meaningless. The second assumption is that 'truth' denotes a relationship of correspondence between the proposition and the real world. A language that is logical in this sense is a language that expresses propositions which, in as much as they are truthful, denote the 'facts' of the real world. The central concern of the positivist for 'verification' rests upon its being verified by observation of the 'real' world.

Now any such language will inevitably fail to capture the nature of love (whether it be erotic or educational). A student's love of learning cannot be a fact in this sense; it cannot be denoted and verified. The language of love is fundamentally connotative rather than denotative. It draws upon images and associations rather than propositional logic. It is poetic rather than technical. We are drawn to enquire into its meaning, rather than to test whether it exists.

This influence of positivist thinking, however, extends beyond an emphasis upon propositional logic and the duality of truth and falsehood. Further dualities emerge based upon the assumed duality of language/reality: subject/object; theory/practice; ought/is; mind/body; intellect/emotion; outside/inside; and so on. With each duality, the question is how does one side of the duality *correspond* to the other side, from which it is conceptually separate. It is difficult to escape from such dualistic structures in thinking. They are deeply embedded in most writing about higher education: research/teaching; process/content; academic/manager, and so on.

Some writers, such as Irigaray (1991), have even argued that the dominance of positivist thinking and dualistic language reflects conceptions of the male body and the male/female duality as conceived by the male. Such male sexuality is organized around the dualistic theme of penetration from outside (active/male) to inside (passive/female). This close relationship between language and the sexual body is suggested in Winterson's title *Written on the Body* (1993), and Peter Greenway's film (1996) *The Pillow Book*, both of which, in different ways, attempt to reach beyond the duality between a language (of love) on the one hand, and the love of which it speaks on the other.

Dualistic thinking might be criticized as being fundamentally analytic, and what we need is a more creative or synthetic approach, but to argue in this way is self-defeating, because it makes the case against dualism on the basis of yet a further duality: that of analysis/synthesis.

A text that can speak of educational love must be one that resists dualistic thinking. It will not restrict itself to observable facts in a supposedly real world. An enquiry into learning that is written in this way strongly challenges the 'evidence based' approach to developing teaching. While evidence plays an important part in enquiry, writing that attempts to understand such a value as the love of one's subject has to go beyond the evidence.

Such writing would acknowledge its openness to different interpretations. In this way the reader would be given precedence over the author in matters of interpretation; or rather, the author would become yet another reader of the created text. As an author of a diary into one's teaching and the problems that arise from it, for example, entries can be returned to and texts reinterpreted in the light of more recent experience and insight. Once written, as Barthes (1977: 143–8) put it, 'the birth of the reader must be at the cost of the death of the author': there are only readers who may then go on to write more texts. This becomes important when one writes reflexively about one's practice. As I hope to illustrate in Chapter 7, the subsequent interpretation, or reading, that we make of our own writing can profoundly influence our understanding of the truths and values that underlie it.

The kind of writing in which we attempt to resist positivist assumptions might employ irony rather than be locked into literalism, thereby resisting the demand that it should stand in a relationship of *correspondence* with a supposedly 'real' world. Any claims it made to be 'theoretical' would always be ironic, recognizing that 'theories' are not structures of propositions corresponding to a real world of facts, but stories that help illuminate our experience. An enquiry into one's educational values, for example, might be such a story, which would embody our personal educational 'theory'. It can be re-read and re-told as part of the process of coming to understand our values more deeply.

Using the term loosely, such a story would help us to clarify our 'philosophy' in order to put it to better effect in our teaching. The philosopher Richard Rorty goes further and views all philosophy – and all science, for that matter – as just 'another kind of writing': it is a story-telling, if you like, with no absolute claims to truth (Rorty 1982). This, presumably, applies to his own philosophical writings as well. So what are we to make of Rorty's 'story' about how science is just about telling stories? Is this itself just another story? Side-stepping this conundrum, the question for us is how can we communicate our ideas to each other? In what sense are our stories about, say, our educational values, any more than *mere* stories? How can we learn from each other's stories?

In trying to answer this question it is tempting to fall back on the custom of referencing, for this is how, in 'academic' writing, we contextualize our research. I have just mentioned Rorty, to whom I have referred the idea of truth not being absolute. Earlier I made reference to Foucault in relation to how language can constrain us. My viewpoint about how 'the erotic' can be reduced to mere technology might have been referred to Marcuse (1969), and so on. What is the significance of this naming? The usual rational explanation given for this academic procedure is that I am thereby locating my text, helping the reader to know what concepts the text draws upon, or acknowledging my debt to these writers. These writers have created know-ledge (concepts, theories, and so on), which is 'out there' to be found in the libraries. By locating my text in reference to theirs and to their fields I am objectifying it; giving it a defined place in the outside world of knowledge.

But is there an 'outside world' of knowledge that can be authoritatively located? There are only texts open to different interpretations. The authors are 'dead' and we are all readers, even of our own texts. Acknowledging this, I realize that any reference I make, say, to Marcuse and his concept of 'the erotic', can only be tentative. After all, do I (or you) really know how he used the concept of 'the erotic'? Or, to be more precise, there is no 'real' understanding of Marcuse's concept of the erotic, and the question becomes whether my reading of his concept conforms to other readings. And for the purposes of this text (which does not purport to be a critical review of Marcuse's work) this may not be very important. So I am left with an uncertainty: should I 'reference' this piece of writing? To do so might offer little help to the reader while lending a spurious authority to the text. To fail to do so could indicate an arrogant unpreparedness to acknowledge my indebtedness to others. To be sure, many disputes and controversies in the academic world – in particular the arts and human sciences – revolve around competing claims over the interpretations given to key texts. It may be that in attempting to reference writing about our own educational values we are more likely to obscure rather than illuminate their nature.

Another way our writing about our work can resist attempts to *denote* and categorize is by means of playfulness, humour and openness, thereby en-gaging the reader in ways other than the purely rational.

I recall, for example, a prospective student coming to talk with me about the possibility of her joining a Masters course that involved some under-standing of philosophy. She was Spanish. The joke here revolves around a confusion between 'translation' and 'explanation'.

Fieldnote 9

'The only trouble is,' she said, 'my English is not very good and I don't think I will understand the technical words the other students use.'

'This will certainly be a problem for you,' I replied, 'but if you can pluck up the courage to ask them to explain when you don't understand, you may find that they don't either, or that attempting to explain themselves will help them to understand better. Take "postmodernism", for example. I challenge anyone to explain that one slowly to someone who is not too familiar with the language.'

'¿Posmodernismo? ¡La traducción es tan fácil!'
['Postmodernism? That's an easy one to translate!']

I was left feeling uncertain about the nature of her difficulty and how her difficulties with the language would impede her understanding. More seems to be involved here than merely translation.

Against the strait-jacket of positivist and academic forms of writing, metaphor, metonymy, and ambiguity are to be welcomed. They undermine the attempt to *denote*, categorize and prescribe relationships of *correspondence*. We are no longer obsessed by concerns with defining our concepts, but attempt rather to illuminate them by connotation. Who, for example, ever learnt anything of significance about learning or loving by *defining* these concepts? Reflecting on and writing about learning should preserve or create an openness, which is a fundamental part of the practice of learning, rather than the closure of categorization, which has more to do with oppression and control.

Writing in this way expresses an intellect that is not afraid of its emotional aspect; an aspect that is particularly important when we come to write about our values. It resists the attempt to create the false duality between the emotions and the intellect that impoverishes the imagination. It does not attempt to cover up or rationalize feelings in an attempt to free the text from so-called subjective bias, but would acknowledge the interplay between the feelings of the writer and reader.

Take the following lines from Wordsworth's Prelude (1975: lines 360–1), in which he describes his feelings when, as a child, he took a rowing boat out at night and rowed across Lake Windermere towards the mountains on the opposite side of the lake:

It was an act of stealth
And troubled pleasure

(Wordsworth 1975 edition: 135)

Viewing the young Wordsworth as a learner, this line captures the quality of his absorption in the learning experience – his own sense of agency in the face of uncertainty, and pleasure in the face of danger – which is beyond the scope of positivist language. It is a *precise* rendering of experience: *rigorous* in a sense that suggests possibilities for writing about learning. To talk of active learning, study skills, student-centredness or other such technical 'educational' terms in relation to this kind of experience misses the point. It misses the point because such terms cannot contain within them the ambiguity and contradictoriness that are captured in this line of poetry, and that are at the heart of the learning experience. This is the kind of stuff of which our student's 'love of the subject matter' is made: acts of troubled pleasure, rather than measures of student satisfaction! It is not a prioritizing of the 'affective' domain as against the 'cognitive' – as the psychologists would dichotomize it – but a recognition that feelings and reflection are bound together in a state of awareness that is rich in potential for loving and learning. To cast Wordsworth's 'act of stealth and troubled pleasure' as an educational objective simply makes no sense: it won't submit.

Like poetry, fantasies and dreams also refuse to submit to analysis simply in terms of denotation. They remain open to differences in interpretation, to ambiguity and uncertainty, and yet can be a powerful expression of learning. In Fieldnote 10 I recorded a dream that had potential for exploring some important aspects of my teaching. This took place during my first term as a lecturer.

Fieldnote 10
This is the dream I had last night.

I had got halfway through a lecture when I realized I had no clothes on. The students didn't seem to have noticed; at least they appeared not to. Then I saw my clothes in a pile at the back of the lecture theatre. They were neatly folded. Shall I go and get them? Or will this draw attention to my state? Then I awoke.

Reflecting on the dream, it was open to many different interpretations, but it seemed best just to stay with the images. The final sense I was left with, from the dream, is that my feelings of vulnerability are not a problem to anyone else, but only to me. That somehow made my fears easier to live with. But there are other ways of viewing the dream. What are the folded clothes? Why were they at the back of the hall? Does my nakedness in this context suggest anything about my relationship with my students? All powerful images for further reflection.

Thinking later about that dream and the questions it raised seemed to do more for developing my awareness of my values and my confidence as a lecturer than a course in teaching skills. It tapped into the deeper levels of fears and desires, which went beyond the evidence of a real teaching session.

The kind of educational enquiry that might start at this point has to be tentative, speculative and risky. In this way it evades the positivist obsession with truth. Henry Miller valued the diary as another appropriate form to which we should look 'not for the truth about things but for the expression of this struggle to be free from the obsession for truth' (Hassan 1987: 9). This gives a new meaning to the idea of a research diary.

I have just begun here to indicate an approach to using language that might enable us to begin to speak of such things as 'the love of learning'. Perhaps we could go further. Rorty (1982), for example, urges us to move beyond the Enlightenment hope that culture can be 'rationalized' or 'scientized' towards one that as a whole can be 'poeticized'. Such a culture would certainly be one in which we could enquire into teaching and learning in greater depth without reducing all questions of educational value to technical accounts of skill, competence and other measures of performance.

My argument in this chapter might seem to be a proposal for enquiry or research into teaching and learning to be viewed less as a science and more as an art. To some extent this is so, and it is not a particularly novel idea. In the 1970s, in his book *The Educational Imagination*, the educational critic Eliot Eisner wrote: 'It is, perhaps, the evaluative aspects of educational criticism that most clearly distinguishes the work of the educational critic from that of the social scientist. Education is, after all, a normative enterprise' (Eisner 1979: 201). It is important, however, not to get drawn into another false dualism: that between science and art.

Significantly, it is a philosopher of science, Feyerabend, who makes perhaps the most cogent case against empiricist method and captures something of the feel for forms of enquiry that offer the kind of alternative perspective I have in mind here. He says we should be 'prepared to initiate joyful experiments even in those domains where change and experimentation seem to be out of the question' (Feyerabend 1975: 17). It is also an eminent scientist – a professor of neurology – who, in his fascinating best-seller *The Man Who Mistook His Wife for a Hat*, warns us of the dangers of science, which 'eschews the judgemental, the particular, the personal and becomes entirely abstract and computational' (Sacks 1985: 19). It is not a case of the arts against the sciences, but the realization that the human cannot be reduced to the mechanical.

Returning to the sentence that concluded Peter's dissertation – 'I want to inspire in my students a love of their subject' – perhaps it is this sense of 'joyfulness', risk and even playfulness, rather than a narrow concern for systematic method and computation, that we need to reclaim in our writing about learning and the values that underlie it. We may then rediscover the heart of our professional identity and resist the dreary oppression of this technical age. Love may then find ways to speak of itself.

7

Reflections on a Story

Introducing the story

Writing stories, poems and fantasies may seem to take us a long way from the detailed observation and analysis of teaching that might more readily be associated with educational enquiry. This approach, which has been called 'fictional-critical writing' (Winter 1991) and 'stories at work' (Bolton 1994) has attracted growing interest as a means of developing professional practice in a number of professions. With a background in engineering and philosophy, it was an odd experience for me to start writing fictionally in order to explore my practice. It required a radical step away from the kind of writing I was used to. I also started with an immense block, feeling that I would be quite incapable of writing a story. It was, however, a very powerful means of enquiry into some difficult issues that arose in my own work as a university teacher, as I hope to show in this chapter.

The 'work' here was not teaching in the normal sense of teaching students, but collaboration with colleagues from a different university, in a different country. The purpose of this collaboration was to support the development – or rather the transformation, as they would have put it (National Commission on Higher Education (NCHE) 1996) – of teaching methods in their institutions in South Africa. My part in this work was to contribute to these changes from my own experience in the UK. As soon as I became involved in this work in a country that was in a state of considerable social upheaval, I was led to question my own identity as a white outsider faced with a cultural context I found difficult to understand. Apartheid was officially dead, but its legacy remained.

While the events that I describe in this chapter seemed far removed from my normal work in my own institution, the process of writing proved to be a powerful strategy, which I have used in more everyday settings. Furthermore, the issues of identity, race, difference and power that the story raises have proved to be important questions for me to consider in a context of

teaching that increasingly includes students and colleagues who are different
from me in important respects.

The first part of the chapter is in the form of a story. Like many stories, it
draws heavily upon actual experience. This will become clear in the second
part of the chapter. There I return to the story, a year or more after it was
written, in order to reflect upon it, reinterpret it and consider what I learnt
by writing it. A final postscript will emphasize the links between this and
some of the major themes of the book.

My process of writing the story began when I arrived at my office in
Sheffield University one morning, having recently returned from South
Africa. Waiting for me was an email from Brenda, a white South African
colleague from the University of the Western Cape. She recalled some
anecdotes I had shared with her about my first responses to being in South
Africa immediately before and after the elections that led to the first African National Congress (ANC) Government. She knew I was interested in
writing fiction as a way of exploring difficult feelings and ideas. At that time
I had made several visits in connection with British Council funded projects
to develop university teaching there. This presented particular problems in
South Africa now that access to higher education was being extended to the
vast majority of the people who had been denied adequate education under
apartheid. Brenda asked me if I would write something for an academic
journal she was editing about my experience in South Africa, using fiction
as a research method.

My immediate response was one of panic. Yes, I really should be able to
do this, but the trouble was I had nothing to say. This was the overriding
feeling I had as a result of my visits. It is such a complex country. Whenever
I had a thought about it I soon knew it was wrong. And in any case, who was
I to say anything of value about this difficult, turbulent place?

I paced up and down my room and, for no apparent reason, picked up
Khalil Gibran's book *The Prophet* (Gibran 1923), which happened to be lying
next to my desk. I opened a page at random, and two thoughts struck me
after reading this page: one was that this had something to say to me; and
the other was that I must say something about my inability to say anything. My
problem of having nothing to say was not a reason for *not* writing. In fact,
being lost for words was the very thing I need to write about, and this extract
from *The Prophet* would, I was sure, help me. It seemed to speak to my own
troubled feelings about teaching in a context of violent political turmoil.

I copied out the extract. I then imagined myself reading this on the
aeroplane on leaving South Africa after my last visit. The story began to
take shape as I recollected the events of this last visit.

Lost for words: a story

And the priestess spoke again and said: Speak to us of Reason and
Passion.

And he answered, saying:

Your soul is oftentimes a battlefield, upon which your reason and your judgement wage war against your passion and your appetite.

Would that I could be the peacemaker in your soul, that I might turn the discord and the rivalry of your elements into oneness and melody.

But how shall I, unless you yourselves be also the peacemakers, nay, the lovers of all your elements?

(Gibran 1923: 58)

Emerging from two hours of dozing, I wriggle uncomfortably in my British Airways economy seat and bring out a pocket version of Kahlil Gibran's *The Prophet*. Opening a page at random, this passage strikes me. Half dreaming, I've been trying to bring together discordant images from the past two weeks in South Africa, aware that in ten hours I'll be back in London, back to the micro-politics of the education department, and the banality of a tired Tory government. A moment to relive, to research my memory . . .

'Excuse me. Coffee, sir?'

'Er . . . yes please.'

. . . that night last week. It was warm and airless as I wandered down towards the Durban sea front near where I was staying. My friends tell me this can be a dangerous thing to do late at night. They also say it's a notorious pick-up spot for gay men.

From the grassy patch beside the kiosks came the heavy beat of music. It drew me towards it, and took me back, back to something before words, back to a pulse that I had almost forgotten but could now hear in my stomach. As I approached I saw women and children and a few men dancing around their stereo set up on the grass. The music drew me closer, absorbing me into the dance. But I couldn't join the others. It wasn't my party. I'd be a gate-crasher . . .

'Black or white, sir?'

'White . . . I mean, er, black. No, yes black, please.'

. . . a white gate-crasher. A circle of dancers had formed, but I stayed on the fringes, my calf muscles tensing and relaxing to the beat of the music. The dance came to an end and a new rhythm started up. The circle of dancers moved left, then right. A woman and her child unlocked their hands and turned to me. They beckoned me into the circle to join the dance. They taught me like a child – except the children here needed no teaching – forward, back, right, left and around, listen, listen, listen to the feel of the beat in the blood.

The rhythm reminded my knee of an old injury, and soon I needed a rest. Two women and their children smiled at me as I limped away. The men's glances were more reserved. I walked around the grassy area near the sea. Small groups of men were talking quietly together some way from the dancers, but obviously belonging to the same party. As I passed a knot

of four, one of the men turned to me, then turned back to his friends.
I could feel them talking about me. Who was I? Who am I? . . .

'This is your captain speaking. For your comfort, will you please fasten
your seat belt.'

. . . The fear of being excluded as a white gate-crasher returned. I was
about to wander away, but had to overcome the fear, get back to the pulse
of the party. For a moment I was held still between leaving and joining.
Then the same man turned back towards me. His face appeared softer.

'Hello. Been enjoying the music?' he said.

'Thanks, yes. Hope it's alright me joining the party. Sometimes I find it
difficult not to dance.'

We exchanged names between the four of us and the ice was broken.
Outside, now inside. Funny how powerful small talk can be. Jabulani, who
was standing opposite me, then interrupted the friendly chat. Looking
straight into my eyes he said:

'I'm sorry. I'm really sorry.'

'Sorry? Why? What are you sorry about?'

'I really am very sorry,' he repeated, looking up at the stars. 'If there's a
God up there, I hope he'll forgive me.'

'Jabulani, what are you saying? Why are you apologising?'

He explained. There had been trouble on the beach front the previous
night. Something about plain clothes police and a fight. Perhaps they'd be
back. He was worried about the women and children. He thought I might
be from the police. He and his friends had been watching me for the past
half hour and were suspicious. You can't be sure of the whites around here,
not at this time of night anyway. But now he realized that I was all right.
There was no need to be afraid.

'I'm really sorry I thought those bad things about you. Now I'm glad
you've joined the party. Lets shake hands again.'

That special handshake – one, two, three. Shaking away fears.

A little later, the group moved off to get a beer. Jabulani put his arm
around my shoulder and walked me towards the sea. We chatted about the
election, about Jo'burg where he worked, and about change. I asked him if
he had been to university. From his look, he obviously thought this an odd
question and shook his head. I bit my tongue and wished I hadn't asked.

'Do you write poetry?' he said.

'No. Well, yes, but not really for anyone else to see.'

'I would love to be a poet. Would you like to hear something I've
written?'

I said I would, but felt anxious. I never know how to respond to someone's poetry. Especially when it's bad.

Jabulani took his arm off my shoulder and we stood still, facing the black
sea with its white fringes of surf rolling towards our feet. We were alone
now. The light breeze died. Jabulani took a step forward and stopped again,
his back towards me. He shuffled and cleared his throat. Then, holding his
head up, he recited slowly, articulating each word with precision:

'A man
Walks towards the waves
Stands
A shot sounds out
He falls
And everybody watches.

I was amongst them.'

I couldn't say anything. I didn't need to. We stood still for a silent minute. Jabulani's guilt was his gift to me. I had not realized that guilt could be black as well as white.

I touched his elbow lightly and we returned slowly towards the dance music and his friends. As we approached, I turned to speak to him.

'Jabulani . . . ? Jabulani. . . . ?'

But he had vanished.

'This is Chris Jones, your captain here again. We shall be turning off the cabin lights so those of you who wish to can get some sleep before we arrive in London. I hope you have a comfortable night.'

I shan't sleep. Words keep returning: words that don't work, dry words from an afternoon a few days later. The conference had just ended . . .

Lisa, Mpho and I are talking with Ahmed about his paper on Recurriculation. Between cigarettes, Lisa reduces her second beer mat to tiny pieces which she drops, one at a time, into her ash tray.

'Oh come on, Ahmed, what's all this *recurriculation* stuff? Why don't you just call it *curriculum* change?'

'But don't you see? We're not just talking about change. It's transformation we need. Our whole curriculum is founded upon power relationships of the past. It's not just a matter of making it *better*. We have to question its very basis, to escape from the relationships of power that it recreates. Take our students. They come from disadvantaged backgrounds, and their schooling further disadvantages them . . .'

Mpho winces and looks into his glass of beer. How does it feel to be named 'disadvantaged'? Who names 'them'? Mpho glances at me as if to signal his exclusion from Lisa and Ahmed's argument. But Ahmed carries on . . .

'. . . getting them to be *critical*. That's what it's about.'

Lisa puts down the remains of her beer mat.

'You mean like deep instead of surface learning?' she adds helpfully.

'No, I don't. I mean *critical*. It's about *emancipation* – you know – Habermas and his *knowledge constitutive interests*. It's about freeing our students from the constraints of authority, ignorance, tradition and so on.'

'Mm . . .' Lisa looks deflated and unconvinced. But then she hasn't read Ahmed's earlier paper on critical theory.

She struggles on with Ahmed. Mpho twiddles his thumbs significantly, then goes up to the bar for more beer, glancing over his shoulder at me. I join him.

'What's all this *about*, then? We don't need Habermas to tell us about oppression. And all those references Ahmed always makes to Aristotle and his concept of *praxis*. Well, we know that Aristotle had no trouble justifying slavery. What do these people know about our struggle? And what's Ahmed doing slapping Lisa down with all this academic theory, as if she were his little student? And in the name of emancipation! It's ironic.'

I can't speak. I don't know. I'm sure Mpho's right, but I don't know. I don't know about the struggle. I don't *know* about Habermas. But I don't think he joined the student uprising on the streets of Paris in 1968? And whose struggle is *our* struggle: Mpho's, Lisa's, mine? Who are 'we'? And all these words. Thick, heavy words. I'm sure Mpho's right. But I can't say.

The bar is crowded now. A few people at the far end are dancing. The music I hadn't noticed before. It's that rhythm, the same dance I heard at the beach party. I look towards our table. Someone is standing behind Ahmed, his hands on Ahmed's shoulders. I recognize him. It's him! Yes it is, it's Jabulani. How did he get here? He's bending over whispering something in Ahmed's ear. Surely Jabulani doesn't want to talk about Habermas. I can't hear what Ahmed is saying, but he glances over at Lisa and then up towards Mpho and me, seeming to beckon us over. As we approach the table Ahmed gets up, Jabulani takes him by the arm, and the two of them make their way over to join the dancers. I lose them in the rhythm of bodies . . .

'Good morning ladies and gentlemen. This is Chris Jones your captain. I hope you've had a good night's rest . . .'

. . . Oh God, where was I? No, it wasn't quite like that last week. Not quite. I never did see Jabulani again, and I'm still looking for his voice. Until I find it, there is little I can say.

Easing my stiff neck, I notice that my book, *The Prophet*, is still open on my lap at pages 58 and 59. I read:

> And if it is a fear you would dispel, the seat of that fear is in your heart and not in the hand of the feared.
>
> Verily all things move within your being in constant half embrace, the desire and the dreaded, the repugnant and the cherished, the pursued and that which you escape.
>
> These things move within you as lights and shadows in pairs that cling.
>
> And when the shadow fades and is no more, the light that lingers becomes a shadow to another light.
>
> And thus your freedom when it loses its fetters becomes itself the fetter of a greater freedom.
>
> (Gibran 1923: 59)

Later reflections

It was now over a year since I wrote the above story in an attempt to understand some of the problems I faced as I collaborated with South

African colleagues in a project to develop university teaching. I will now reflect upon this story in an attempt to show what I have learnt from writing it.

What Khalil Gibran had to say in the opening extract seemed to be the issue for me. Somehow reason – and I often think of myself as being good at using that, I am after all an academic – didn't seem to serve me in trying to understand my difficulties with South Africa. My experiences there had often provoked strong emotions in me, but I couldn't find the words to describe these emotions, and I didn't really know where they were located. Apartheid had just come to an end, but the pain that had been left in its wake remained, together with the joy of new possibilities for the people. But why did these feelings strike me so sharply? I was not, after all, South African. Yet somehow the pain and the joy overwhelmed me as though it were mine. Did it remind me of my own unrecovered pain? Or my own guilt? Or my own fantasies of a joyful freedom? Who was I in connection with these experiences? Were my own roots entangled with those of the oppressors, or could I identify with the oppressed? I am white. But what does that really *mean* in the context of a new multicultural South Africa recovering from apartheid?

The story represents my thoughts, recollections and imaginings as I reflect upon past events in the aeroplane. For me, aeroplane journeys provide a kind of airlock between one reality and another. Planes and airports sterilize culture; they have a kind of meaning that strips away meaning. Cultural artefacts, like the ethnic souvenirs in the duty free shops, seem to hang there, suspended in a vacuum that separates them totally from their origins, stripped of any cultural meaning they may have had. And the same is so for me when I am suspended in the air. There I was, separated from my roots, to which I was returning, and separated from this other world, which I had now left behind. The prospect of the depression and banality of my own home country struck me here – perhaps a symbol of my own depression – whereas the new South Africa held out the possibility of something else: the possibility of emerging at last from a long ache that had been with me as long as I could remember. Was it South Africa's ache; or was it mine?

The sequence of events that opens the story concerning the dancing and the party is exactly as I remember it taking place. As I walked down to the beach front, I remember the warning of danger that my South African colleagues would often offer. Why do so many of them warn me of the dangers of walking on the beach at night? I sometimes imagine they even *liked* giving me these warnings. They are caring for me, yes, but I wonder if there is something else behind that care. Is caring always a motive to be suspected? Is it a fear? Not just a fear for my safety, perhaps, but a fear of something else.

So the beach front is a gay pick-up spot. But what's the significance of 'gay' in this context? Are 'gays' more dangerous than 'straights' when they're on the pick-up? What I could readily see was that the people who congregated there at night were predominantly black. Oh yes, I had read in the papers the facts about the many recent murders and muggings in Durban. Everyone had their tales of violence to tell me. I did need to be careful. But the warnings I had been given by white colleagues evoked in me not so much the fear of danger, of the unknown and of difference, as the *legitimation* of that fear. Was this my colleagues' fear or mine as well? A fear of black, a fear of gay? Was this at the root of their racism, my racism? This first episode of my story is exactly as it really happened. Fiction is sometimes superfluous.

My story then switches into 'real time' as I am offered coffee by the black steward. I recall a feeling of guilt when I tell a black steward that I prefer white coffee. No, that's not true. I actually prefer black coffee on aeroplanes, especially when the milk offered is UHT. But I would feel guilty if I said I preferred it white. No that's not true either. It's just that I feel the question is ambivalent. I feel interrogated, as if I'm being asked to justify my being white. Or am I being challenged to confront his blackness? The contortions of a guilty mind. I can see why they've now taken to asking whether or not you want milk, rather than whether you prefer black or white.

The story now returns to the beach party. While I was dancing with the women and children my own anxieties about being an outsider seemed to evaporate as we became joined in the music. The woman and child who unlocked their hands – and their treating me as if I were a child – to me symbolized the strength of innocence and its power to overcome fear, thus enabling me to learn the dance from them. But the music was more than just an external presence that I could engage in with them. What is important is the way I interpreted the music. In fact, I don't think the music was especially African or ethnic. Hearing the same music on Radio 1 in the UK I would have been unmoved by another piece of rock pop. Like most popular rock music, it has its roots in African culture. But in this context, it connected with my preconceptions of being African. Had these preconceptions of mine anything at all to do with the party as experienced by the dancers, or were they merely an indication of my own stereotypical assumptions about Africanness? There seems to be some connection here between my African stereotype of rhythm, darkness, the belly as the seat of passion, and my own childhood and things dark and forgotten, but also warm and embracing.

As I leave the warmth of the women and children who taught me their dance, and move among the men, my own fears of darkness return. The captain's voice, telling me to fasten my seat belt, disturbs my reverie and warns me of the danger I felt as I walked among the men.

My fears again disappear when I am confronted with the ordinariness of the interaction with Jabulani and his friends and the traditional three-stage handshake. Some years ago I gate-crashed parties at home, and the experience was always accompanied by a certain amount of tension as I wondered whether I'd be found out. But this was different. Here a more menacing fear was alternating with a feeling of warmth. Does what has been going on in my head really bear any relation at all to the events? Have I not been totally screwed up by my own fears, the fears of my white friends, or my own racist prejudices? And does this not, perhaps, all connect back with something deeply about myself and my own unrecognized pain, mixed up with a yearning for warmth, which has nothing at all to do with South Africa or its struggle for liberation?

Again, I want to emphasize that this and the rest of the scene on the beach front are as accurate a rendering as I can give of the events and my response to them at the time, which I noted down before going to bed at the end of the evening. The only exception is Jabulani's name. I couldn't recall his name, although I did recall that he came from Johannesburg. Being unfamiliar with African names in that region, I asked a friend who came from Jo'burg to suggest some different names for this character. Jabulani was one of the names she suggested. Meaning 'joy', this name seemed altogether appropriate for my story, for I imagined that underneath his feelings of fear and guilt, which this episode recounts, lay a deep sense of joy. By the end of the story I hoped to have understood something about that joy.

Jabulani's apology to me is perhaps the most poignant moment in all my visits to South Africa. I suddenly realized the recursive nature of fear; how fear breeds fear. I had been afraid of these men on the beach front, and so had wandered around feeling uncertain. This behaviour had been interpreted by them as being suspicious and so fuelled their fear of me. So they talked about me, and this made me more fearful. But once I had plucked up the courage to overcome my fear, and they had done the same, the cycle of fear could be dispelled and I could come to the realization that while I had been afraid of them, they had been afraid of me.

The grace of Jabulani's apology for having been suspicious of me was indeed remarkable. Was I not the one who should apologise, I remember feeling, apologise for being white? This takes us back to the old issue of White Guilt, a term that is often used to describe the response of white liberals to black oppression. Everyone knows about White Guilt in South Africa, but it is a silent guilt. I want to address it in this story.

Perhaps guilt is often a manifestation of hidden fear, or fear a manifestation of hidden guilt. But these feelings of guilt are often merely side-stepped by my white colleagues when they talk of the rising crime rates and the warnings not to go down to the beach at night. It is as though it is all right to talk about being afraid of crime, but not to talk about being afraid of blacks.

I have recalled Jabulani's poem exactly as he told it to me as we stood beside the sea. I was astonished by his own feelings of guilt, no less than his earlier fear of me. It reminds me of reports of feelings of extreme guilt on the part of Jews held in concentration camps during World War II, as they saw their friends being taken to the gas chambers. It is not only the oppressors who experience guilt.

At the time of the story, the Truth and Reconciliation Commission, set up by the ANC Government, was investigating the crimes of apartheid. It stood as a public symbol of the need to face fear and guilt. But how is this to be addressed at a personal level? I could begin to make my own sense of it through the direct experience retold in the story. How much more powerful was this than a chat over a beer with a friend, or a laboured intellectual piece of writing. This was more than just a sharing of feelings, or an academic investigation. It was a stark confrontation with my own fear and guilt through the 'storying' of an experience that initially seemed powerful, but whose power I was only later able to realize and understand. The writing here enabled me to bypass the need for rational connection and argument. As the characters emerge, they could tell me through the story.

I had been disturbed by an intuition that my responses to South Africa were connected to my own history rather than to South Africa itself. Now this connection was becoming clearer. It had to do with my own feelings of guilt about a lot of personal things that have nothing to do with South Africa. I was already aware of the feelings of guilt, but not of the fear. Where was the fear? What was the pain that was at its root? The exploration of these questions is vital to me, but outside the scope of this story. What I had achieved here was some sense of what was mine and what was not mine: a kind of boundary between me and South Africa. Without this clarity there was a danger that my perceptions would be romanticized by connecting with my own struggles rather than with those of South Africa. This awareness could make it more possible for me to establish the identity I needed in order to work effectively as an outsider in South Africa attempting to collaborate with colleagues to develop university teaching.

The movement to the second episode of the story is marked by the captain's invocation of sleep. In this I further develop my doubts about the value of rational argument, especially when this comes in the form of imported Western academic discourses. Their use may do more to continue oppression in another form, rather than to emancipate the oppressed.

The imaginary conversation in the bar between Mpho, Lisa and Ahmed did not actually take place, but is a reconstruction from a number of different encounters that took place around a conference. I brought them together here to develop the story. It reflects my dilemma in my work with those who are concerned to transform the relationships of teaching and learning in South African universities. On the one hand there is the concern to bring South Africa into the international academic community, with all that implies about adopting the discourses of Western academia. On the other, there is the struggle to Africanize, expressed by the voices that have for so long been silenced. This case for an Afro-centric curriculum, founded upon Africa philosophy, is made by Ndaba (1996).

Between the two sides of this debate there seems to be a third position, which draws upon the critical social theory of Western (largely German) social theorists. It is in this context that Ahmed talks about Habermas and his concept of 'knowledge constitutive interests'. He is probably referring here to Habermas's texts *The Theory of Communicative Action* (Habermas 1984, 1987), which he draws upon in his insensitive dismissal of Lisa's contribution about 'deep' and 'surface' learning (see Richardson *et al.* 1987). It seems to me that this position – what Ahmed calls critical theory – is underpinned by an essentially modernist or 'Enlightenment' view that rational argument can help us to understand and replace oppressive social forces by a more just set of social relationships. Such a view has been a powerful force in the drive towards democracy in the developed world over the past 300 years.

But I have two worries about this approach in the context of South Africa, which concerned me here. In the first place its roots are in centuries of European thinking and lack any historical connection with the thinking of black Africans. In the second place, the approach assumes that rationality is an absolute and universal quality. This would be disputed even by some white philosophers, broadly described as postmodern, who see reason as just another way of storying. I don't want to get into this difficult philosophical debate here, but in my story I wanted to explore some of the feelings that are mixed up in it, and how oppressive behaviour so often seems to survive critique unscathed. When Mpho leaves the group to go over to the bar, he is not only rejecting Ahmed's hypocrisy (evidenced by Ahmed's sexist dismissal of Lisa), but also his theoretical resources, which, Mpho feels, are the product of the very white culture that was the cause of the oppression of Africans.

At a personal and professional level, the story again raises the question of what intellectual resources I have to offer in this situation. While I am prepared, in a rather unscholarly sort of way, to enter the academic arguments that are alluded to by people like Ahmed in the story, I am still left feeling 'but I can't say'. I am, however, beginning to get some sense of what are my problems (fears, guilts, and so on) and what are South Africa's. It feels as though I am able to establish for myself some kind of boundaries between my self and the place as I experience it. With this clearer sense of identity, I can perhaps now begin to address this question: 'Who am I to say anything?'

When Jabulani appears on the scene and then goes off to dance with Ahmed, there is a hint of his being gay. In the light of my recollection of his physical warmth towards me when he recited his poem to me by the sea, I feel positive about his sexual orientation. Sexual orientation is not an issue I was wanting to explore here in any depth. For me, it rather stood as a symbol of the kind of *difference* that, like race and gender (or discipline, for that matter), is a site of prejudice. My feeling good about his sexuality reflects my also feeling good about his blackness. Both are sources of warmth. The way he intrudes into this scene is an attempt to express the way in which his insight, his kind of knowing – his joy, even – can cut straight through the kind of academic discourses that concern Ahmed.

When Mpho distances himself from the whole debate by going over to the bar, he is humiliated by Ahmed's implied description of him as disadvantaged. I see this as a central problem in any 'development' work, and particularly in South Africa with its apartheid history. For one group in society to be naming another group as 'disadvantaged' so easily serves to reinforce the very power relationships that are at the root of the problem. This point is very concisely made by the (then) Vice-chancellor of a historically black university in South Africa (Ndebele 1995). It so easily becomes a rationalization for the powerful group defining what constitutes 'advantage' and therefore the developmental needs of the so-called disadvantaged. I have experience this problem particularly acutely in South African higher education. The quite proper concern to give black students more equal access to higher education so readily leads to students who have been oppressed by apartheid being judged 'disadvantaged' by those from more privileged sections within academia. This in turn leads to the view that it is the students who need some remedial treatment rather than the institutions themselves.

Although this problem struck me forcefully in South Africa, it is in fact also a problem in the UK, where questions of widening access to higher education are accompanied by notions of 'disadvantage' applied to some sections of society, such as the disabled. But this is not a simple matter. In South Africa I didn't want to be making negative judgements about those who have suffered the oppression of apartheid; nor do I want to judge, from my own safe distance, those who are genuinely trying to bring greater justice to their society. Here I am only attempting to understand how Mpho might have felt hearing Ahmed's arrogant depiction of disadvantage.

Ahmed here also represents a legacy of the apartheid past. Apartheid sought to rule by dividing the racial groups. Ahmed – who, as his name suggests, would have been described by apartheid as being Indian – does not identify himself as being as disadvantaged as African groups to which he refers. His arrogance, which he interestingly expresses towards Lisa – a female white, not a male black – leads me to wonder whether questions of gender are at stake here, as well as race.

I might have expected Jabulani to identify with Mpho in this matter. I'm sure he also would not like to be named as being disadvantaged. But no, with Jabulani's extraordinary insight, such debates are merely academic. They don't really connect with the passion which he feels and is expressed in his poem. This can cut through prejudice. Unlike Mpho, he can't be hurt by Ahmed's intellectualizing, and its arrogance passes him by. He wants to dance.

Mpho's invitation to Ahmed to dance expresses the power of love in the struggle between reason (represented by Ahmed) and passion (represented by Mpho). And this takes us back to the opening extract by Kahlil Gibran. Of course, I was not aware of the subtlety of this form in the story when I wrote it. The story created its own form and logic. That is the power of storying.

In my story, this second episode in the bar comes to me in the form of a dream, whereas the first – which took place on the beach front – was in the form of a recollection of my experience. This shift between reality and dream within the story parallels the shifts between fact and fiction in my own experience. We are accustomed to drawing rigid boundaries between our dream world and our waking world, and between our imagination and our perception. But these distinctions and the boundaries between them are permeable. Perception is also an imaginative act, and the imagination is always fed by perception. Many of the greatest scientific discoveries (Archimedes' Principle, the benzene ring, the pneumatic tyre and so on) were made from insights gained during dream-like states of consciousness, in which the boundaries between reality and fantasy were traversed. The power of story writing – which allows for fictional rendering of experience – is that it enables us to move back and forth across these boundaries.

It was by using such a method, in which I could make these transitions, that I could begin to make the distinctions between my self, which was perceiving South Africa, and the South Africa that was being perceived. In this way the enquiry fulfilled a role rather like the supervisor or the therapist: it enabled distinctions to be made between my 'baggage' as a professional worker and that of my client group. Having begun to make these distinctions – principally between my own feelings of fear and guilt and those I encountered in South Africa – there is now some chance that I would not impose my own feelings inappropriately upon those with whom I collaborated.

The story concludes with the page from *The Prophet* that faced the page I had picked at random that started the story. The coincidence seemed extraordinary. But is this really a coincidence? Or does it not suggest the power of our own concerns and preoccupations to interpret imaginatively the chance perception? I have certainly found that when I am able to free myself from the normal rational ways of thinking, and have opened myself to more speculative, playful and imaginative processes, serendipity can be a source of insight. The form of the 'found poem' – a poem made up of phrases taken from seemingly unrelated contexts such as signs beside a road – is a creative strategy of this sort that creates meaning out of chance.

This extract from Gibran's *The Prophet* expresses the limitations of dualistic thinking, which separates the observer from the observed, and the fearful from the object of fear, as well as the feared from the desired, and freedom from constraint. For the philosopher Hegel, dialectical thinking concerns the ways in which opposites provide the basis for moving on: the struggle between thesis and antithesis leads to synthesis. What Gibran reminds us here is that once we have emerged into the new position – the synthesis – we become entrapped in yet another dialectical opposition: 'And thus your freedom when it loses its fetters becomes itself the fetter of a greater freedom'. In the context of a South Africa freed from the dialectical opposition of black/white apartheid, the new situation can be one in which a greater freedom is fettered. Similarly, students freed from the authoritarian control of the didactic teacher, may emerge to face a new set of constraints, which their new-found responsibility forces upon them.

In terms of this process of fictional writing, the real and the imagined are not in opposition but are 'in pairs that cling' like light and shadows. By storying my experiences in a way that did not bind me to truth (as in the sense of conformity to the events), I could come closer to being able to act in a way that is more true, in the sense of being straight and unencumbered by my own unresolved baggage and prejudice.

Postscript

The original events to which the story relates took place in 1995; I wrote the story in 1996; and my reflection upon it was first sketched out in 1997, and developed further here in 1999. But this is not the end of the story. These reflections on my story constitute yet another story, another text to be reinterpreted, another set of 'research data' to be further analysed. Such further reflection might take me deeper into my own still unresolved personal feelings of guilt and fear; or it might take a different direction altogether and focus upon the place of 'critique' in the South African context; or it might provide the basis for further thinking about the differences that I encounter in my more normal teaching in a UK university. Each successive interpretation is refracted through intervening work and experience, and from a distance and angle that are always shifting.

In the same way, reflections upon the more everyday experience of teaching change through time. What once seemed like a successful piece of teaching later appears to have been limited by my own unexamined assumptions. There are no 'best practices' in teaching; no fixed data of evidence. All is open to interpretation and re-interpretation as contexts shift and we learn from further experience and reflection. This is why anyone committed to enquiring into their teaching will be suspicious of those who claim to bring solutions. It is also why we need to explore and reappraise our values as we attempt to teach in ways that manifest them.

Another factor that can radically alter my perspective on my story is the reflection of other readers upon it. Just as there is a time to move from the interactive aspects of enquiry described in the earlier chapters of this book, to the private reflective space of writing, so it is important to move outwards again from this private space to a more public one. That, after all, is in the nature of academic work: the move between private scholarly activity to the public critique of students and peers through teaching and publication. That is what I am doing in presenting my own enquiry here to a critical audience.

8

Exploring Values in Teaching

Introduction

Improving teaching involves critique, personal enquiry and openness to change. Without these, skills alone will not equip us to make sound educational judgements in the changing and often unpredictable circumstances of teaching.

Enquiring into our teaching inevitably leads us, at some point, to address questions about our values. It has been suggested that the whole purpose of enquiring into our practice as educators is aimed at answering two questions: 'How do I improve what I am doing?' and 'How do I live my values more fully?' (Whitehead 1993: 7). But coming to know what our values are is part of the process of putting them into effect. In Chapters 6 and 7 I considered how writing can help in this exploration. Here I want to look more closely at the problems and consequences of exploring those of our values that are relevant to our role as teachers and learners.

In Chapters 3, 4 and 5 I explored the nature of enquiry when it is supported by teachers from different disciplinary backgrounds meeting to learn from each other. I proposed a model for this process that describes how interaction between colleagues working together might draw upon three contexts of knowledge: the public, the personal and the shared context of their work together. What distinguishes this from more traditional approaches to learning is the emphasis upon the shared context, where individuals address the present process of how they are working together – their values in action – and reflect on the ways in which they are learning from each other. This is a reflexive process. It enables one to challenge the theoretical resources from the public context, and the practical experience from the personal or professional context, by testing out these ideas and experiences against the present circumstances of working together.

This approach often leads to questions of value being addressed in ways that can be very direct. For example, the issue of gender equality is important, not only in those subjects, such as engineering in the UK, in which women are traditionally under represented. It may involve questioning whether, or how, female students respond differently to male students; or whether male teachers treat female students in the same way as they treat male students; or how men and women relate differently in a group setting; or even how the very subject matter – say engineering or nursing – is influenced by the predominance of one gender, and so on. Such discussion might be informed by the media, policy documents or popular and research literature in the public domain. It is also likely to draw upon people's personal experiences.

Once the discussion draws upon the shared experience, however, its impact becomes much more direct. For now, we are not just dealing with, say, 'men' and 'women' as abstract categories, or simply sharing our past experiences of gender relationships. Now we are dealing with the immediate present of how the men and women in this group are perceiving their interactions with one another to be influenced by gender. Are we, for example, making assumptions about each other on the basis of gender? Do the women and the men in the group feel they have an equal opportunity to contribute? Is the proportion of women to men a significant factor in how we are working or the concerns we are addressing?

An environment of trust and support is crucial if questions such as these are to be explored in any depth. Such issues readily lead to feelings of vulnerability or embarrassment if people are expected to give each other honest feedback about how their contribution is perceived. They may even feel hurt or angry if individuals are not supportive and sensitive to each other's feelings. If an appropriate context is provided for these emotions to be faced and explored, however, the interaction may appear to be more like therapy than educational enquiry, as people risk exposing feelings they would normally keep to themselves.

Is some kind of therapy involved, then, as part of enquiry into teaching? And if initial and continuing development of academics is to be a compulsory feature of a university career, is some kind of compulsory therapy involved? Can it be justified to expose people to this kind of enquiry? On the other hand, how can I develop my practice in order to discover my values and live them more fully unless I am prepared to be open to hearing how others perceive my values *in action*?

In Chapters 6 and 7 I have indicated that the process of writing, particularly if we can escape from some of the narrower notions of 'academic' writing, can provide a means for exploring and articulating emotions and values with a view to bringing our practice of teaching into closer alignment with those values. This kind of 'care for the self' (Foucault 1984) can help us to become more authentic and integrated in our actions. In her book *The Therapeutic Potential of Creative Writing*, Gillie Bolton shows how the very process of writing can be a therapy that helps us to face the 'fears and horrors buried inside which cause problems' (Bolton 1999: 11). Teaching is a human activity that involves the whole person. It might be supposed, then, that in relating as teachers to our students and colleagues, such 'problems' need to be addressed.

In this chapter, I want to start by seeing if we can draw some distinctions between the kind of learning about values and feelings that is an appropriate part of our enquiry as university teachers, on the one hand, and a wider and more personal and possibly therapeutic engagement, on the other. Barnett, in a review of my earlier book *The Enquiring Tutor* (Rowland 1993) asks:

> to what extent is it legitimate to frame a set of experiences on an advanced course in which such exposure of deep personal feelings is likely? . . . The case, therefore, for causing students [who in the context of this book would be university teachers involved in their professional development] to confront their own values and emotions, their own personal characteristics and capabilities, with all the potentially disturbing consequences . . . needs to be *made*.
>
> (Barnett 1996: 154)

I now want to consider some of the issues involved in making this case.

Values, freedom and psychotherapy

Teachers and psychotherapists have at least one thing in common. They are both involved in a process of changing someone else's (the student's or the client's) behaviour. But so are politicians, military commanders, religious evangelists and prison governors. What, then, is it that distinguishes teachers and therapists from others who try to change people's behaviour?

The answer, I think, has to do with some conception of agency or freedom. For being responsible for one's learning implies being a free agent in it: freedom implies the exercise of choice. It is an old adage that a teacher can no more force someone to learn something than force a horse to drink water. Equally, it is a truism among therapists that the therapist cannot 'cure' someone of their problem, but only support the client in 'curing' themself. Military commanders, gaolers and politicians can force people to change their behaviour; so, perhaps, can teachers and therapists. Indeed, both often use, and at times abuse, their power in order to change the way their students or clients behave. But they cannot force *learning* upon their students.

Carl Rogers was a writer on psychotherapy and on teaching. His most influential book about teaching and learning was, significantly, called *Freedom To Learn* (Rogers 1969). He was an important exponent of 'student-centred learning' and 'person-centred therapy', and very influential in what came to be known as 'progressive education' in UK primary schools. In his work, the responsibility of the individual for their own learning, and therefore their freedom (as a client in therapy or as a student), is paramount.

In the philosophy of education, there has also been a concern to articulate the relationship between education and freedom, which can be traced back to Rousseau and even Plato. More recently, the American philosopher John Dewey – one of whose books was called *Freedom and Culture* (1939) – was arguably the most significant educationist of this century. He emphasized the relationship between education and freedom at two levels: first, that education's *ends* are concerned with creating a more free and democratic society; and second, that the *means* of educating even the youngest child should emphasize their freedom in learning from their experience of the world. As far as adult learning is concerned, Paulo Freire (1972b), in *Cultural Action and Freedom*, made the case for adults taking control of their own learning rather than being passive recipients of it. In the preface to this book, João da Veiga Coutinho writes: 'Education is either for domestication or for freedom' (Freire 1972b: 9). But if freedom is the *end* that learning serves, it must also be reflected in the *means* by which these ends are achieved.

While freedom has been an underlying theme of education in general, university teaching has been much less informed by insights from psychotherapy. A notable exception is Jane Abercrombie (see Abercrombie (1993) for a useful collection of her work). As a teacher and researcher in zoology (at Birmingham University) and later in medical and architectural education and educational management (at University College London), she was also very involved in group analytic methods. Group analysis is concerned to explore how individuals learn in a group, the dynamics of their relationships, the role that the unconscious plays in this process of personal learning, and how it might be 'facilitated', 'led' or 'conducted'. She applied group analytic methods to work with students and lecturers as a way of helping them to act more effectively. An important part of these methods is the kind of 'free' or 'associative' discussion that is to be found in psychotherapeutic groups. Impressed by her experience of group analysis as used in a psychotherapeutic group, she says: 'This was an illuminating experience for me, and I felt that if one could transfer to a teaching group something of the atmosphere . . . established in this therapeutic group, new ways of seeing and thinking might be encouraged' (Abercombie 1993: 64). Of particular concern to her was that learners should be much more free from dependency upon their teachers.

Such an approach suggests a role for the facilitator (or 'conductor' as Abercrombie would put it) that is not authoritarian and permits a free flow of ideas between participants. This approach is consistent with the role of the group facilitator as suggested in Chapters 3–5. Like the model I have proposed, it aims to optimize the opportunity for participants to communicate their subjective perceptions, feelings and experiences, as well as engaging with a public field of knowledge. The structure of such group discussion is therefore one that emerges, rather than being predefined by the facilitator.

To describe such discussion as 'free', however, is not to say that it is *laissez-faire*. A *laissez-faire* discussion would be characterized by a lack of challenge, with difficult intellectual or emotional material being readily side-stepped; a tendency to avoid anything too risky. A *laissez-faire* approach would have no means of ensuring that enquiry drew upon all three contexts of knowledge in order to develop critical perspectives. Freedom in group discussion, as in any other form of social action, is the proper basis for critical engagement and responsibility, not a licence for an easy life.

In the following fieldnote extract from work with a group of lecturers on our Masters course, I describe a situation in which I intervened in order to prevent what I believed would have become a *laissez-faire* discussion. In doing so, the group interaction became more like a therapeutic group, as one of the participants observed.

Fieldnote 11

Lin facilitated the session. She first gave us time briefly to re-read the text on small group work (Jacques 1989: 4–22), which she had suggested should be discussed at this meeting. After some silent reading, the discussion ranged around fairly generally. I began to feel rather frustrated that we were not getting anywhere. We were dealing with questions as abstractions rather than as concrete experience. There were a number of assumptions that this text made that were not being challenged, and I was uncertain about how best to promote a more critical engagement.

Then Robin turned our attention to our own process. Commenting on how Jacques's article discussed different arrangements for seating in a small group teaching situation, he drew our attention to the fact that we were all sitting around a large table. 'Wouldn't it be better if we got rid of the table and sat with a more intimate arrangement of chairs?' he said.

Someone made a joke about intimacy and there was some gentle laughter at Robin's comment, but the discussion returned very soon to a wide ranging conversation about group work, as we continued to sit around the large conference table.

I was irritated by the way Robin's question was just avoided. It seemed to me that his insight of considering Jacques's paper about organizing group work in the light of our own work here as a group was altogether appropriate. Furthermore, I felt it was unacceptable for people to be ignored in that way (not that Robin seemed upset). After about three minutes, I said, perhaps a bit severely: 'Robin asked what I thought was an interesting question, does anyone want to answer it?'

There was a silence, which I was not inclined to break, although I felt increasingly aware that I was expected to, and embarrassed that my intervention had been rather 'teacherly'. Then Robin said something about the seating arrangements again. There was a discussion about the merits of having a table to work on, or being in a more intimate setting with chairs in a circle. It was suggested that perhaps the table symbolized a kind of boundary or defence of our personal space. Very soon a decision was made and the table was removed and stacked away and the chairs rearranged in a close circle. We took our seats again. There was another silence as we got used to our new arrangement.

Then someone asked how we had made that decision. Bob said that he thought although I had done no more than remind people that

Robin had asked a question, by doing this I had exercised my power as tutor and had manipulated the situation for us to move. He did, however, prefer the new arrangement, he said. Robin, on the other hand, said that I had not manipulated anything but had merely supported him by asking people to respond to his question.

Now that the group were thinking about their own shared experience of decision making, someone else commented about how our conversation included more moments of silence now that the table had been moved. Someone said they felt comfortable with that silence. They went on to ask Hugo and Christina (for both of whom English was not their first language) how they felt about the fact that they were both often very quiet during our meetings. Christina talked about her uncertainties being not so much a language problem, but a lack of experience of teaching. She said she was younger than others in the group and was not sure what she had to contribute to the understanding of others.

The quality of the discussion was now quite different from that of the first part of the meeting. Perhaps this was because we were now seated more intimately, with the table providing less of a barrier; perhaps because we were being reflexive about our work together. Statements were often followed by brief silences, as if people were taking in and digesting what had been said. There didn't seem to be any need to fill these spaces. For me, it seemed that we were now listening more carefully to each other. Perhaps this explained why Christina was now able to be very open about her own insecurities about our work together. I think she felt supported by people's encouragement, particularly when someone said how much they valued her contributions, even if she didn't speak much, and that she shouldn't feel pressured into saying more if she didn't want to.

Towards the end of the session, Sam commented that he had deliberately kept silent for half an hour, just to see what that would be like and to observe. He was, he said, very rarely prepared to be silent, and the self-imposed discipline of not speaking was, he said, very illuminating. He said that he felt that the session was now much more like a group therapy session. He said he wanted to give some thought to his question of whether the learning process is a kind of therapy.

The meeting concluded with Russell offering to 'facilitate' the next session on the subject of the role of silence in teaching. Someone joked that he wouldn't have to say much about that. I felt the joke was altogether fitting.

My intervention of reminding people that Robin had asked a question was crucial (but not more so, of course, than Robin's question itself) although I had not said much during this session. No doubt Bob was right in saying I had exercised my tutorly power, and I can understand him experiencing this as manipulation, even if he did like the change. From my own perspective it was not manipulative since it was in accordance with an understanding that I had thought we shared (although in fact we may not yet have) about how the group should function. This understanding involved first the requirement that we should listen to each other, and second the importance of legitimating anyone's perspective about the shared context of our work together. I felt that by in effect ignoring Robin's question, the group had broken both of these implicit ground rules. But perhaps it was only through the experience of the session that these rules became explicit. The group had never formally negotiated any ground rules, and I was aware of the difficulties in doing so (as explored in Chapter 5).

This particular session was often referred to in the discussions of the group over the next months as signifying the moment when the quality of their interaction changed. It seemed that at that point we made concrete the value of respecting each other's choice to contribute verbally, or not, as we wished. This value could not be merely legislated for by an agreement to observe a ground rule. We were thus more prepared to listen to each other, to tolerate and even enjoy silence as an opportunity to think about what was happening and to learn from each other. From then our work together was much more characterized by what Abercrombie terms, 'free', 'analytic' or 'associative' group discussion (Abercrombie 1993: 63–7).

This draws upon some psychotherapeutic insights about communication and group processes. But there are differences between this and group therapy. The first relates to the purposes of enquiry: what is it we are trying to learn about? In teaching students biology, for example, associative discussion can have great value, but the subject matter is biology. Learning about how to communicate effectively, how to behave in accordance with our values and how to work as a team, are aspects of learning that are valuable in all social settings. Many studies purport to show how discussion promotes this kind of learning (see, for example, Abercrombie and Terry 1978). Such kinds of learning have come to be termed 'transferable skills' and it is often said that these skills should be developed on all courses. But as long as the curriculum is biology, then any such learning is subordinated to the purpose of learning biology. The subject matter of biology (knowledge in the public context) largely structures the activity and inevitably limits the extent to which students should be investigating their personal values and emotions, although they do have a place.

When the subject matter is our own teaching and we or our colleagues are the 'students', however, the limitations imposed by the subject are much less clear, for the subject matter is now much more than just the public knowledge of, say, educational theory, although that plays an important part. To a much greater extent than for the biology student, the subject matter for the enquiring teacher *is* their ability to communicate, to relate to others and to make moral choices based upon values, for this is what teaching consists of. Thus working in this field is likely to draw upon the kind of reflexive and self-critical attitude to our practice that may be informed by a group analytic or pyschotherapeutic approach. However, the practice at issue here is our practice as *teachers*, not our practice as lovers, mothers or consumers. Our values about justice or the nature of truth are important here, but our sexual morality, for example (up to a point), is not relevant. The subject matter of our enquiry, therefore, is only a limited aspect of the subject matter of personal therapy.

This boundary between the purposes of enquiry as a teacher and the purposes of psychotherapeutic enquiry is not absolute. In Chapter 7, for example, through my writing about my uncertainties of working in South Africa, it *was* important for me to explore my feelings around race and guilt and to examine my own values about these. I was involved there in widening university access to black people in a post-apartheid university system in which power was still largely held by white people. My writing, although therapeutic, was concerned with issues that seemed to me to impact directly on my professional work. I did also, however, write more than the text in Chapter 7. In the process I discovered something about how my feelings related to early childhood experiences and other present personal difficulties. Such writing was also therapeutic, but it was intensely private and was not related, in any way I was able *or concerned* to identify, with my public practice as a teacher. It was, so to speak, 'another story', for myself only. Bolton (1999) has shown how creative writing of this sort can have an enormous impact as a form of self-therapy, and in this kind of private writing I would want to say, with Bolton (1999: 11), that this writing was for me, a gift to myself, rather than a means to my professional development. But this distinction is not a clear one. Being a teacher involves the whole person: the boundaries between personal development and professional development, and between the private and public, are permeable. Change is likely to involve questioning such boundaries.

The second distinction I want to make between therapy and learning relates to the appropriate forms of collaboration involved. Collaborating with colleagues to enquire into teaching can take many forms. It may take place between two colleagues who have worked closely together; or a more junior teacher and a mentor as part of an induction programme; or a short course; or an extended course in which a group of people meet over a period of years. It may be informal and voluntary, or a formal requirement for probation. Each of these contexts can offer a different degree of support. The support may be provided by someone in the role of a tutor, facilitator or mentor; it may arise from a kind of co-counselling arrangement; or access to an academic or professional network; or it may merely be a matter of the opportunity provided by a close friend and colleague. Making a judgement about the degree of support that is available can be an important part in assessing the potential depth of the enquiry and the kind of personal exposure that might be involved.

I recall an occasion when I believe I made a radical misjudgement about this question of support. I ran a residential two-day experiential workshop on self-directed learning (along the lines reported in Rowland 1993: 56–86). The workshop was designed to explore how we make decisions, communicate and collaborate in our learning. It was organized in such a way as to encourage people to learn about their motives, feelings and strategies for dealing with others by exploring how these issues emerged within the shared context of their work together (rather like in a T-group (see Smith 1969)). Inevitably, this involved a large degree of emotional involvement and exposure to difficult feelings, which required trust between the participants. Although the participants were in no way 'patients', the workshop was in many ways more like a therapeutic experience than an academic one.

At a follow-up session a week after the workshop, many of the participants reported very positively on what they had learnt about themselves from it, and how it had helped them to change their approach in dealing with students, colleagues and those who had power over them. One participant, however, was absent from this meeting. I failed to follow this up immediately. It was only some months later when I tried to contact her, and failed, that I learnt, through a third person, that the experience of the workshop had disturbed her very considerably, and that she had since left her job and was now suffering depression. Of course, I could not judge to what extent these unfortunate events were caused by the workshop, and thus to what extent I was responsible. It may be that the workshop had uncovered, or in some way brought back to her, deep-seated personal problems that I could not have known about and that were not directly related to her professional work, but it did seem to me that had I followed up her absence immediately and attempted to support her in dealing with her disturbed feelings that arose from the workshop, these events might have been averted, or I could have helped her to seek professional therapeutic support.

What I learnt from this – possibly at the expense of this unfortunate person – is the extent to which support is needed if academics are to explore the deeper aspects of themselves that shape the way they behave as teachers. What also became clear to me is that such support may need to be founded upon a greater experience than I was able to offer. I was not a trained counsellor or therapist and, as such, it is important to acknowledge the limits of the support I could offer. Accordingly we need to recognize that there are limits to how far down the road of personal exploration we should expect to go with colleagues.

My argument, then, is that university teaching in general, and educational enquiry on the part of university teachers in particular, can usefully draw upon therapeutic insights. Indeed, the model I developed in Chapter 4 has some parallels with group therapy in the way it encourages people to address their present feelings about their relationships and values within the shared context. Its purpose, however, is not primarily therapeutic, and the kinds of support normally available are likely to be more limited both in terms of time and professional therapeutic expertise available.

The exploration of our values and the attempt to live them more fully in our teaching is not, however, just a matter of personal or inward looking enquiry. They are influenced by the social, cultural and political circumstances in which we teach. It is to these that I now want to turn.

Values and society

'Only beings who can reflect upon the fact that they are determined are capable of freeing themselves' (Freire 1972b: 52). Here Freire is speaking in the context of the so-called Third World, and from the perspective of teaching that aims to free people from oppression. For him, 'conscientization' is the process of reflecting upon the social conditions that determine us in order to act upon them. As university teachers, perhaps in the First World and at the beginning of the twenty-first century, we may not think of ourselves as part of an oppressed group. In many respects, and certainly in relation to the Central American rural population with whom Freire worked, our conditions of life and work are among the most privileged. Nevertheless, we experience pressure to conform to externally imposed requirements that may be driven by political and social agendas that are not our own. These influences act not only on our behaviour, but also on our values. Educational enquiry, as I understand it here, involves reflecting on these influences in order to play our part in acting on them in our struggle to free ourselves in order to act more educationally with our students.

Working with colleagues, students and institutions from different cultural settings often enables us to perceive the ways in which social conditions shape our own – as well as other people's – educational values. Such cultural 'distance' can bring differences in values into more prominent relief.

With the increase in global markets and the possibilities for communication made available by new technologies, university work is increasingly attempting to transcend cultural divides. The effect of globalization, however, is often to hide cultural differences in teaching by denying that teaching is informed by cultural values. This denial is achieved by perceiving teaching as if it were devoid of values and merely a mechanical or technical activity whose 'standards' can be objectively quality assured. Teaching, we are led to believe, will then simply play its part within the uncontested values of the global market. Technically sophisticated courseware then becomes a marketable product whose value – or rather price – is assumed to bear no relationship to cultural values. In order to counter this, I think it is important for this enquiry to focus a little on work with those whose values emerge from different cultural settings.

I have found that such contacts, like the following, have enabled me to see the extent to which I cannot take my own educational and cultural values for granted.

Fieldnote 12

A colleague asked me if I would read Fatima's assignment as part of a Masters in Educational Studies. He was unhappy with her work, but did not know how to help her. I read the essay and agreed to talk with her about it.

When I met Fatima, we started by chatting about life in the Middle Eastern country that she comes from. I had just returned from Brunei, and mentioned my impressions of life there. In the course of our conversation I told her I was impressed by the employment available to women there, how they all drove cars and how they appeared to be free from much of the sexist advertising which is so dominant in the West. She said that in her country women could not drive cars. I asked her how she felt about this. She looked at me as if this was a silly question and replied: 'Of course we can't drive, because you can't see properly when you're wearing a yashmak.'

We went on to discuss her essay in much detail. I asked her to elaborate on a number of points, indicated what I saw as weaknesses in her argument and suggested how this could be improved. I made some jottings in the margin to indicate the points we had discussed. After an hour of concentrated discussion, her tutor joined us. He asked her if she had found the meeting useful. She said: 'Well we've had a long discussion of my essay, and I can see it's wrong in many ways, but I've not been told what to say to make it right.'

What struck me here was not Fatima's lack of knowledge, but what seemed to me to be a total misunderstanding – from my point of view – about the nature of academic work. From her perspective, her task was to write what was correct and that if she didn't know what was correct, then the tutor should tell her and she would learn. I think she felt that I was being unnecessarily obscure or awkward in not saying exactly what she should say at those points where she 'had gone wrong'.

Now this kind of dependence upon the teacher will be familiar to teachers of undergraduates. But how could she have got as far as a Masters degree course and yet still be so misguided about the nature of academic work? For me, the clue was in her comment about wearing a yashmak. It would, of course, be unsafe to drive while wearing a yashmak, but my questioning how she felt about this did not lead her to question this constraint. Indeed, she may not even have seen it as a constraint, and thus thought my question silly. She merely pointed out the logic of the situation: that if you do wear one, you can't see well enough to drive. When it came to the discussion of her assignment, she was no more likely to question her view that I knew what it would be right for her to say in her essay, than to question her tradition of wearing a yashmak in public.

It was easy to view this tale from my 'Western' perspective, to be critical of Fatima's lack of intellectual ability and to disregard the coherence of her own Moslem traditions. It reminded me of an earlier occasion when another Moslem student on the same course confronted a similar problem about authority. This student had completed her dissertation. In the final part of it she was expected to reflect upon the validity of the research methodology she had adopted. In doing this, she had concluded that since her research findings were consistent with the teachings of the Koran, her approach must have been valid. For her, the validity of her work *consisted in* its congruence with religious teaching, rather than its rational secular basis.

In these instances, the use of reason is subordinated to a higher authority: the authority of cultural tradition (in respect of wearing a yashmak), or of the teacher (in respect of writing a correct assignment), or of religious teaching (in respect of the appropriateness of research methods). While I do not share these values, would I be right to impose my own upon the student's framework of belief? Or, to throw this question of cultural values into even sharper relief, was not my belief that reason and argument should predominate over religious or other systems of belief, an assumption that is open to question? Of course, I could respond by stating that since she is taking part in a degree offered by my university, she should abide by the criteria and assumptions that underpin academic work in this institution, but such a response is merely to replace the authority structure of Islam, with which she identifies, by that of my university, with which she may not.

I shall not attempt to resolve this dilemma here. As I noted at the beginning of Chapter 4 in the discussion of educational theory, there can be no final *reason* why rationality should prevail. The issue does, however, underline the fact that even my most fundamental ideas about teaching and learning are culturally informed. That, of course, includes all the ideas that have informed this enquiry. This does not invalidate my educational enquiry, but on the contrary helped illuminate the ways in which my own practices of teaching could be viewed very differently under changed cultural circumstances.

We live in society in which change is endemic. Often changes are spoken of as though they were led by advances in science and technology. Such advances are indeed likely to change radically the ways we relate to students. What is more difficult to see, however, is the ways that changes in political and social values impact upon our teaching. If, as I have claimed throughout this book, teaching is an activity informed by values and is an expression of them, then we should expect to see changes in teaching to reflect these broader changes in social values.

Russia and South Africa are both countries that have undergone enormous social upheaval over the past two decades, from very different historical backgrounds. During the Soviet era in Russia, university teaching was designed 'to instil in students a particular moral, social and political world view' (Avis 1996: 59). This view was based upon a reading of Marxist-Lenism that underlined the importance of ideological instruction in order to prepare students to play their role in the centralized communist state.

During the apartheid era in South Africa, university teaching, especially in the historically black universities, was informed by what has been called 'fundamental pedagogics'. This is an authoritarian approach to teaching and passive approach to learning that served the objectives of the apartheid state.

These two approaches to teaching – the Soviet Russian and apartheid South African – were different in important ways. The Russian system emphasized community involvement and responsibility; the South African system emphasized white supremacy. What these systems shared, however, was the subordination of the 'democratic, open relationships' between teachers and learners that are fundamental to democracy, to the higher authority of the state.

Recently, each has undergone change reflecting an increased concern for democratization. Whatever our conception of 'democracy' – and no doubt this is differently understood by British, Russian and South African people – the close relationship between education and some conception of freedom and therefore democracy, is an important one.

> Democracy is founded on faith in the power of 'pooled and cooperative experience'. Through democratic, open relationships, as opposed to autocratic and authoritarian ones, however benign, we learn from and with one another. We can know things in this way, in combination with one another, that we cannot know alone. Unless democratic habits of thought and action are part of 'the fiber of a people', Dewey writes, political democracy is insecure.
>
> (Blake *et al.* 1998: 100)

We might therefore expect that as these societies move towards more secure democratic forms of organization and values, university teaching will change to reflect a greater concern for students' freedom as democratic participants in their own learning.

Working with colleagues in these countries, both in the UK and in their own institutions in Russia and South Africa, has helped me to understand this connection between teaching and democratic values. In both countries, moves towards the more active involvement of students in their learning are viewed as part of this process of social transformation. In South Africa, a range of academic freedoms and the encouragement of democracy were specifically written into the preamble to the first democratically elected government's Higher Education Bill (ANC 1997: 1); and in Russia the requirement for more 'active methods of teaching' in the social sciences was recognized by the USSR State Committee for Public Education even before the final demise of the Soviet system in 1991 (Avis 1996: 60).

Even where change towards more democratic values is supported at the level of national policies, however, change at the classroom level is anything but straightforward. In a brief article on introducing 'active learning' methods in an interdisciplinary Masters course at a Russian university, Kirpotin, a professor of botany, explains how these changes had to overcome the expectations of 'shy' students who were not used to contributing their own ideas, and lecturers who were used to relating to their students in more authoritarian ways (Kirpotin 1999). Trying to effect similar changes in teaching at a historically black university in South Africa, the problems of overcoming the legacy of the authoritarianism of 'fundamental pedagogics' have been found to be even more profound (Ruth 1996).

Values and the discipline

In this discussion of values I have deliberately drawn a close relationship between the social values of freedom and democracy, on the one hand, and more open and democratic relationships between students and teachers on the other. Accordingly, I have rejected the idea that our enquiry into the practice of teaching is a *value neutral* science.

On my first visit to a Russian university, I was somewhat taken aback when I was introduced to staff by a senior academic at the university as being an expert in 'the science of teaching'. At first, the implication of this seemed to me to be that what I had to offer came with the authority of science, as it were untainted by personal or subjective values, democratic or otherwise. According to such a view, developments in teaching towards, say, greater student involvement, have nothing to do with the values of democracy, or any other values for that matter. Such changes, resulting as they may from enquiry into our teaching, are the result of the *scientific* nature of our enquiry. Effective teaching, from this point of view, could as well serve the purposes of an authoritarian communist state as the purposes of democracy.

My introduction, however, was made in Russian and interpreted to me in English. When I later questioned the interpreter, I discovered that in Russian, the term 'science' is often used to describe any scholarly form of enquiry. It seems probable that this reflects the higher status given to scientific over other forms of enquiry in Russia throughout the Soviet era (1917–1991). In this context, describing my knowledge of teaching, or pedagogy, as a science may have signified no more than a mark of respect for it as the result of scholarly enquiry. In the same way, the philosophical disciplines of logic, aesthetics and ethics used to be called 'moral sciences', as is reflected in the University of Cambridge philosophy degree, which still bears that title.

For us as university teachers, however, the description of our practice of teaching as the application of science may be very significant. Our sense of identity comes, to a large extent, from the discipline in which we teach and research. As teachers and researchers of science or economics, science or economics are more than simply the subject matter that the teachers happens to know about. They define themselves – to some extent at least – as scientists or economists. What it means to be an economist is not, of course, fixed, but the power of the academic community in the discipline – the 'academic tribe' as Becher (1989) calls it – is considerable:

> Any systematic questioning of the accepted disciplinary ideology will be seen as heresy and may be punished by expulsion; any infiltration of alien values and practices will be appropriately dealt with ... Thus, within economics, those who question the basic axioms of the subject are regarded as deranged if not positively dangerous, and are liable to find themselves cast into a wilderness of their own; deviants in other

marginal fields, such as statistical areas of mathematics, may be cut off
and left to form an independent self-sufficient community.

(Becher 1989: 37)

This 'disciplinary ideology' – or framework of values – shapes not only how
we research our subject, but also how we teach it. As a university teacher of
engineering, with a background in the natural sciences, Hand shows that
'scientific teaching *and research* is [sic] not (therefore) oriented towards
questioning the underlying nature of the scientific enterprise' (Hand 1999:
123 my italics). To consider such philosophical questions, Hand says, is
often seen as being a waste of time and beyond the concerns of the university teacher or researcher of science.

Now whether or not we agree with Hand's description of the scientific
community, or his criticism of it, he is putting forward a value position that
is at odds with his view of his 'academic tribe'. The implications of such a
value position must be crucial to his teaching. A science teacher who believes that scientists should question 'the underlying nature of the scientific
enterprise' would be concerned to introduce students to ways of questioning from which issues about the philosophical basis of their subject arise.
Those who believed, on the other hand, that science is about the real world
and that such questioning is not relevant, or is the job of philosophers
rather than scientists, would approach students differently.

A similar case can be made for other disciplines. Design, for example, is
not just a subject matter but involves valuing invention, form and function
in ways that have implications for the process as well as the content of
teaching. A teacher of design who did not encourage students to be invent-
ive in their learning would be failing to teach students to become designers.
And in philosophy, for example, Plato describes Socrates as an exponent of
a particular philosophical method, but this Socratic form of question and
answer is also a pedagogic practice.

As academics, our commitment to our subject infuses us with the values
embodied in it. These values, however, are not uncontested. Mathematics,
for example, is understood by some mathematicians as being abstracted
from experience of the world, with value to be judged by its potential for
understanding or transforming the world. For others the validity of mathematics consists in its internal coherence as a pure form. It is the difference
between these two philosophical positions which led to the classical debate
within the philosophy of mathematics over the question of whether it is
possible to conceive of a universe in which the laws of mathematics, as we
understand them, do not hold.

Furthermore, these underlying values are open to change. Recent initiatives in the UK and the USA in medicine and medical education, for example,
are attempting to raise the role of the arts in health care. Sir Kenneth
Calman, then Chief Medical Officer in the UK wrote:

Quality of life for patients and professionals is clearly important. We
need to change our understanding as to how it might be improved

... [by] a broader movement linking the arts (visual, dramatic, literature, etc.) to the physical, psychological and social problems of patients in communities.

(Calman 1999: 9)

Such a movement could challenge the domination that natural science methodologies in teaching and research have held in medical education. Changes of this sort can impact not only upon the social or emotional aspects of health, but even upon the neurological. Oliver Sacks, a professor of clinical neurology, has argued that therapies based in the arts can lead to improvement in brain damage, and that such approaches should not be eclipsed by narrower, systems based approaches (1985: 141–2).

On the Masters course described in the earlier chapters, there have been a number of teachers who, having been introduced to a literature that raises questions about the philosophical underpinnings of their subject, have found that this radically alters the way they orient themselves to their discipline and the manner in which they teach it. The word 'philosophy' comes from the Greek meaning 'a love of wisdom'. Understood in this way, an understanding of the philosophical basis of a subject should be an essential part of any higher education practice, and certainly of any enquiry into university teaching. It is a discipline that helps us to open up to critical scrutiny the assumptions and values that underlie the subject and inform the ways it is taught.

How we understand the nature of our discipline, and orient ourselves towards our disciplinary community, thus involves questions of value that relate directly to our teaching. Even the limiting case of someone who claims that their disciplinary orientation is free from any question of values is making a statement about values that is contestable. It is also making a statement that will impact upon how the teacher responds to the subjectivity of their students. The model I developed in Chapter 4 as an approach towards critical interdisciplinarity showed how such value positions, and therefore disciplinary boundaries, can be opened to challenge by working with groups of teachers from different disciplines.

As university teachers we have a complex identity shaped by our discipline, our personal histories and our social contexts. All of these inform the values that underlie our work with students. Values from these different aspects of our life are not necessarily in conformity with one another. Indeed, our very identity can be understood as consisting of multiple selves, as the psychotherapist Rowan puts it in *Subpersonalities: The People Inside Us* (Rowan 1990). One of the aims of enquiry into our teaching is to come to know these different identities, to bring ourselves into a closer harmony with our selves and thus into more authentic relationships with our students. This is a personal as well as a professional project.

9

What's to be Done?

Introduction

When Chris came into my room, as described on page 1, he complained that I had made things difficult for him; he could not continue to teach in the same way. And now we are at the final chapter, I fear that life may not be any easier for him. I have pursued my enquiry, developed a line of thinking about teachers working together, reflecting and writing, delved into some of the problems that arise and expressed my own uncertainties. I have, I hope, conveyed something of the excitement of learning with colleagues from different subject areas and how the process of developing our teaching can be viewed as a form of research, but it has been clear that there are no quick fixes, no easy solutions to becoming a better teacher. The more we think about it, the more questions we raise, while getting precious little in the way of any answers.

Indeed, I have stressed the need for scepticism in the face of those who claim to have answers, and doubt that educational research will provide solutions to my teaching problems. Teaching and enquiry have led me to question, aware that every solution seems to pose yet further problems. It has been said, and I would agree, that pedagogy – the understanding of teaching and learning – *is* this very questioning and doubting (Van Manen 1988: 447).

University teaching, however, is a life of action. Enquiry and the pursuit of pedagogical understanding can imbue our teaching with insight and a sense of purpose, but we do not work in monasteries where we have endless time to contemplate the subtleties of learning and the meaning of life for ourselves and our students. It is ironic that, in order for me to have the time to put together this enquiry, my colleague Alan took over my own teaching duties for some months. It therefore seems appropriate for me now to address more directly the question 'What's to be done?' in the light of the real pressures that most of us work under: the pressures of student numbers, of accountability to internal and external bodies keen to ensure that standards are improved, and a working environment in which we may not always feel as valued as we would like.

To do this, I shall address a number of quite specific questions, which I imagine a reader, like Chris, to ask having read the discussion of the foregoing chapters. This dialogue will, I hope, serve to draw together the themes of the book while demonstrating that enquiry provides an altogether practical basis for university teaching. It will also shift the focus somewhat towards teaching students, rather than our own professional development.

Dialogue with a reader

You have said a lot about how you learn about teaching. But at the end of the day, the development of your teaching depends upon your being able to detect when it has improved. That means being able to tell when your teaching is successful. How do you know if your teaching is successful?
The obvious answer to this would be that the success of my teaching depends on what the students have learned. I find it useful to turn this answer on its head, however, and suggest that the success of my teaching is best judged by considering what I have learned from it.

But you advocate the value of an approach that is student-centred. The students' interests should be foremost, you value negotiating with them and say learning should develop from their understanding and interests. So how can you say that it's your learning, rather than the students', which gives a measure of its value?
Yes, this may sound paradoxical, since it is the students' learning that provides the whole purpose of my work as a teacher. But it is not really, for two reasons.

First, it is incredibly difficult to know what a student has learnt from a particular teaching session. Obviously this is the case in a mass lecture, but it is also the case in a small group tutorial or even a one-to-one research supervision. I can, of course, ask questions to assess what the students know, or have them solve problems or complete tasks. But I can never be at all sure what of lasting value has been learnt during a particular session. Indeed, learning does not just happen during a teaching session. The session is only a part of a train of thinking – a 'learning cycle', if you like – of experiences, reflections, readings and so on, which contribute to the emergence of a new idea, way of thinking, skill or understanding. I only have to consider how difficult it was for me to judge what *I* learnt from, say, writing the story in Chapter 7, to realize that it is an almost impossible task to make valid judgements about what a *student* has learnt from are particular activity.

Second, I have throughout this book stressed the value of collaboration in learning: collaboration between students, and between students and teacher. As soon as I view teaching and learning as a two-way process of communicating, making meaning – or *enquiry* – then it makes sense to suppose that if the communication is working in one direction, it is also working in the other. That is, if the students are learning from it, then so am I. That's not to say we are learning the *same* things. Much of what a first year mathematics student comes to learn is already, hopefully, known by their lecturer. But much is to be learnt, both about the process of learning *and* about mathematics itself, from observing and listening to students struggling with new ideas, trying to relate them to their existing knowledge and relating this to their wider experience. Even the most ignorant student who is really engaged in a subject, can sometimes ask the kind of questions that challenge my own understanding, as I found out working with 6-year-old children. Look, for example, at *Philosophy and the Young Child* (Matthews 1980). This book is an introductory text for a university philosophy course built solely around the insightful questions of young children. Or, reflecting back on Fieldnote 2 (p. 49) of the discussion about 'What is learning?', I remember thinking how naïve this question was, and was tempted to dismiss it. It was only when I allowed it to be explored that I realized what *I* could learn from it. As it turned out, that conversation initiated my thinking that led to the model that I develop in Chapter 4, but I am quite sure that's not what the *students* learnt from it.

This raises a lot of questions, which we may come to. But first, you mentioned the mass lecture. How can I possibly learn from the students when I have to give 50 minute lectures to groups of 200 students? Your ideas sound fine as an ideal, but how can they work in this kind of situation, in which many of us find ourselves?
Yes it is difficult. We all know that the most boring lecturers are those who give the same lectures each year, from notes they know almost off by heart, with perfect timing and no space for surprises. There may, of course, be the occasional lecture that is perfectly scripted, acted with panache and has the students spellbound, but that is the exception, and not one to which, I believe, I can realistically aspire. Even where it is a successful performance, which the students enjoy, it may well be more an entertainment than an educational experience.

Nevertheless, I want to say that a lecture can be a most valuable resource for learning. Valenta (1974) wrote a lovely piece called *To See a Chemist Thinking*, in which he describes how giving a lecture in chemistry can be just that, a portrayal of the way of thinking that characterizes the discipline of chemistry. Such an approach attempts to engage students in a process of chemical enquiry rather than tell or explain the facts, theories or equations of chemistry.

I think this is a challenging but difficult task. In this article, Valenta says: 'My only chance is to enjoy my own lectures and I believe that the only way I can achieve that is not to know precisely and ahead of time what will happen in any one of them' (Valenta 1974: 54). Here we have Valenta the enquirer: it is only because he does *not* know exactly what is going to happen that he is able to learn from it and enjoy it. I want to take this way of thinking a little further. Before I give a lecture I often ask myself two questions: 'What might I learn from giving this lecture?' and 'How can I arrange things to maximize the chance of this happening?' The answer to this second question usually involves giving some control to the students, perhaps through some kind of paired discussion or more open ended activity. Unless they have some kind of control, albeit limited, it is difficult to see how I am going to find out anything from them I didn't already know. Just asking them questions to which I already know the answers gets me, and them, I suspect, nowhere.

This question of control, or power, seems to underlie much of what you are saying in this book, but my experience of teaching is that I do not have enough control. Control of the curriculum is largely dictated to me by more senior colleagues and professional bodies; control of practical details like time-tabling and exams is usually beyond me; control of my own professional development, it now seems, is likely to be exercised by others; and when I teach it is as much as I can do to maintain control there. And now you're asking me to take less control of that too.

I share your feeling that our control over our professional practice is becoming increasingly limited. Performance measures, standardization, quality control procedures, increasing managerialism and the influences of the global market all serve to limit our professional control. In respect of this kind of control, my own enquiry can help to ameliorate things. It can increase my confidence, help me to create for my students the kind of intellectual space that is threatened by these developments, make me less susceptible to fads and fashions and draw me into more collegial relationships. Enquiry can increase my scope for making educational judgements and thus increase a sense of control.

But when it comes to my students, the boot is on the other foot. In spite of the rhetoric of the student as 'customer', students have little enough control over the process of their own higher education. Without some degree of control, it is difficult to see how they can make their experience of learning meaningful in terms of their interests and needs, which is necessary if they are to transfer that learning to other contexts. Much is talked, these days, about transferable skills and lifelong learning. If learning is to extend beyond the immediate academic context, the student must be able to relate it to their wider experience. Thus some degree of control by my students, and a decrease in their dependence upon me as their teacher, serves both their learning needs and mine, as their enquiring teacher.

Furthermore, control over learning activity is not a 'zero sum game': just because my student has more it doesn't mean that I have less. In Fieldnote 8 (p. 67), for example, the very freedom that I gave to Nigel to make decisions about his course, led to the kind of change in him that I intended, as the teacher, and on which he commented. As I have argued in Chapter 8, freedom and educational processes are inextricably linked, and so if *I* want to ensure that the students have an educational experience, then I must enable *them* to have some control of the process. And once I do that, there is the possibility for enquiry as I investigate how the students use this freedom.

Yes, I can see that this enables your enquiry to get under way. Your teaching now becomes a kind of experiment as you find out about your students' perspectives, the choices they make, how they learn, and so on. I can see that this has educational value for them as well. But what I can't see is how I can use this approach when I have to teach students the basics of their subject. Until they've mastered the basics, they are not in a position to exercise freedom and be creative, are they?

This is one of the most challenging aspects of curriculum design: to plan experiences for students that give them some freedom to make their own interpretations while, at the same time, making sure that important themes are addressed.

The term' basics', though, can be confusing here. It can mean two quite different things: elementary or fundamental. Elementary things are easy and can be done or understood with little insight, knowledge or skill. Fundamental things, on the other hand, serve as a foundation. They can be returned to again and again and understood at ever greater depth. They bring us close to the philosophy of a subject: the understanding of its assumptions and purposes. In arithmetic, for example, counting is elementary, but the concept of a number is fundamental. An infant school teacher might describe a 6-year-old child as 'having the concept of number'. On the other hand, Russell and Frege were still discussing the concept – whether it was the name of a class or of a class of classes – at the height of their mathematical careers (Russell 1946: 784).

The fundamental ideas of a discipline may be widely accepted and uncontested by the 'academic tribe' (Becher 1989) but, as we saw in Chapter 8, they are not fixed. One feature of a higher education is that it should engage the student with the fundamentals of a discipline in ways that enable them to see these ideas, like all other ideas, as being essentially contestable. This, according to Barnett, is an aspect of *critical thinking* (Barnett 1997: 71).

University teaching, then, should engage students in contesting, not just in learning about, the fundamental ideas of their subject. This means allowing them to enter into debate with these ideas.

Fair enough, but how can they do that before they have learnt what these ideas are?
I think they can. A first year economics student can debate the fundamental concept of money, drawing upon their everyday experience. A science student can contest the idea that scientific observation is objective, or a sociology student the concept of social class. These fundamental ideas have very specific meanings within their discipline, as they will come to understand, but right from the beginning they need to view such concepts as being open to contestation. In that way they will see that such ideas are related to everyday experience while, at the same time, they can be refined in order to challenge taken for granted assumptions about that experience.

Debating such things gives them a degree of control and it also gives me the opportunity to learn from their understandings and insights as part of my enquiry. Even their mistakes and misunderstandings – in fact *especially* these – can lead me to critique and clarify my own concepts.

This is why the model of learning involving public, personal and shared knowledge, which I developed in Chapters 4 and 5 places so much emphasis on the perspectives of the participants (as students). For only then can they begin to look *critically* at fundamental questions. It was not a question of learning some supposed 'basic' educational theory first, and only later using it creatively, but rather of encountering in relation to their practice some fundamental questions with which educational theory deals, in order, later, to engage critically with significant texts in the public domain.

This does not completely answer the problem about how to ensure that students learn the elementary procedures, facts and theories of the subject, but it can at least provide a context for learning the basics informed by, and engaging the students with, the fundamental concepts, practices and purposes of the subject. Without this, learning the basics is liable to become a rather tiresome routine leading to superficial learning.

This sounds exciting, but again I am left feeling it is rather idealistic. Given the pressures under which I teach, how can I have the time to enquire into all my students' different understandings and their ways of learning about these things? It's difficult enough to fulfil the normal assessment requirements of marking without enquiring into the details of how my students understand the fundamental conceptions of the discipline in every teaching session. Are you able to conduct this kind of enquiry in relation to all your teaching?

No, of course not. I want to distinguish, though, between conducting an enquiry into my teaching (or my students' learning) and having an attitude of enquiry. Schön (1983) talks about the importance of reflection as a deliberate strategy – a kind of research activity – for improving one's professional practice. This is what I mean by conducting an enquiry. Only a very small proportion of my teaching can be subjected to the kind of analysis I have attempted in this book, given the pressures of time.

The results of such enquiries, however, help me to interpret the situation and make judgements in my normal teaching. They inform my attitude towards my teaching and give it an interest as I am always testing out my ideas. To have such an attitude does not involve spending extra time. Indeed, it can reduce the amount of time I have to spend on planning because I am more sensitive to the situation as it develops and have more confidence to organize teaching along the lines that Valenta recommends, without everything being planned in advance. Teaching that is planned down to the last detail but not underpinned by an enquiring attitude is sterile, but such an enquiring attitude needs to be kept alive by more deliberate forms of enquiry. This can take quite a lot of time. I find it valuable to set aside time for this at the cost of time spent on detailed planning.

How, then, do you choose what aspect of your teaching to subject to this kind of more deliberative enquiry? What should I look at first?

Teaching is an immensely difficult business, and we can approach this difficulty positively or negatively. The positive way is to view it as offering a rich and interesting field for investigation; the negative way is to view it as an endless sequence of almost impossible problems. It is both, but I think that the heart of my enquiry must be my interest, just as with any other intellectual pursuit. I am sure that there are many ways in which my teaching leaves much to be desired. But if I am to develop it, I have to start with what interests me. This approach is, I believe, at odds with the approach implied by many of the pronouncements of quality assurers, bureaucrats and standardizers. Too often, they emphasize weaknesses and shortcomings in their attempt to get us up to scratch. As with any form of learning or research, I want to start from my interests and strengths. That way I am able to maintain and extend my interest. Furthermore, since learning about teaching and learning is a critical activity, I can only pursue it when I am committed to reflecting upon it in some depth, asking awkward questions and being open to change. I can only do these things when I am really interested.

To be realistic, I don't find all my teaching exciting. Some of it is a bit of a chore. But as long as I focus my enquiry on something that really does interest me, then I often find that this leads to my developing this interest in an aspect of my teaching where there had been little before.

For example, I used to view information technology and its role in teaching as being a very dull matter about which I knew little. I had always been interested, however, in the nature of human interaction and its dynamic in small group teaching, so I focused my enquiries on such things as group processes, and not on the role of the computer. Later, a group I worked with became involved in developing their ideas through email correspondence (see Chapter 5, pp. 70–2). I then realized that this was also a form of personal interaction, in some ways similar to, and in some interesting ways very different from face-to-face communication. Then I began to be interested in the potential for computer mediated interaction as part of the learning process. Had I focused initially upon my own weaknesses in the area of new technology, I don't believe I would have developed this interest in a new technology.

That must have been a valuable experience, but in that example you were working with other university teachers. They may have been your students, but they were not like normal students. They shared your involvement in exploring educational issues. How am I to develop an enquiry when my students are maths undergraduates who have no interest in teaching and learning as a subject for investigation? If, as you suggest in this book, enquiry benefits from a critical engagement with other people, with whom am I to engage? Do I have to join some professional development course?

First, a word about 'normal' students. I think everyone is interested in their own learning. Or, at least, they are interested in themselves. Whenever I have shared with a group of students my thoughts about the previous session with them, they are always fascinated, want to discuss it with me, and often have very illuminating comments to make. This encourages them to think about their own ways of learning. It is also well established principle that metacognition – that is, thinking about one's own understanding – is an invaluable part of the learning process. And so it can be valuable for both the students and for my enquiry to involve them in some discussion of their learning.

But I take your point. Our students do not share our responsibilities and problems in teaching. Nor do they have the kinds of experiences our colleagues have to draw upon. If possible, enquiry does benefit from some kind of collaborative context with other staff. Increasingly in universities, this can be provided by professional development courses, or by mentorship arrangements. Some departments have a system of pairing new lecturers with a more established colleague, who has the role of a critical friend who might observe your teaching and whose teaching you might observe. This can provide a useful basis for a collaborative enquiry when the aim is not to be judgemental, but to offer mutual support in investigating teaching. Informal collegial relationships, however, are often the most fruitful.

There is a real problem in developing the appropriate collegial relationships for the supportive yet critical forms of collaboration that are part of enquiry processes. As you showed in Chapter 1, university teaching has come under increasing surveillance, which, together with increased student numbers, modularization and other effects of a more competitive market, has served to fragment our working life. Doesn't this militate against collegiality? I have in mind the endless requirement to prepare documentation for external assessors; to give an account of our teaching so that it looks good; take part in committee meetings about teaching in which we never really explore our teaching. Surely this works against the kind of open and critical stance that characterizes enquiry as you have described it?
Yes, the effects of bureaucratization can certainly undermine enquiry, and the requirement for endless paperwork is soul destroying. This is a problem for research as well as teaching: the emphasis is on measuring the pig, as it were, rather than on fattening it. But I think one can be too negative about this, and too ready to underestimate the intelligence of those who play the role of assessors of our teaching. I have often encountered criticisms of departments' teaching on the grounds that although they have made everything look good, they have not shown that they are sufficiently critical of themselves. As teachers committed to enquiring into our teaching, I really think we have a responsibility here. We have to find ways of articulating our investigations, surfacing the problems that we encounter and demonstrating the positive effects this can have upon the students' experience. Bureaucratic exercises do not encourage teachers to admit their weaknesses, but if we can identify problems (as well as successes) and demonstrate our commitment and strategy for working on them through sustained enquiry, then I think that can be quite impressive.

Let me take, as an example, the often routine requirement for students to evaluate our teaching via some kind of questionnaire. Now questionnaires can have a value, but often this activity, once routinized and standarized, encourages little thought on the part of staff or students, and produces results that – while claiming to be 'objective' – at best provide a measure of student satisfaction, which is not the same as educational value. More often they are not even this and are totally invalid indicators of the students' educational experience. This is an example of higher education inappropriately adopting a strategy taken from market research.

Enquiring into the experience of some of my students has led me to see the limitations of this kind of evaluation, and to explore more reflective strategies (see, for example, Rowland 1993: 124–41). I have a responsibility to articulate these criticisms and suggestions, and to find ways of documenting them and offering them as alternatives to the current procedures. The attempt to make these kinds of changes can be a struggle. Institutional ways of responding to the requirement of accountability tend to be bureaucratic, inflexible and mechanical, but those who operate these requirements are often our colleagues or others who do have some understanding that education is more than a merely mechanical process of knowledge and skill delivery. Part of my task, as an enquirer, is to persuade them of the value of a more thoughtful approach and to bend or change bureaucratic requirements where they conflict with the interests of students' learning. I think that we should not just contemplate and act upon what takes place between ourselves and our students, but also engage with the social situation, which may constrain our students', and our own, learning.

Finally, speaking of our own learning, you have frequently made the point that our learning – our research – and teaching should be brought into closer relationships: that enquiry into teaching is not only a form of research, but that it can draw upon our disciplinary research. That's an exciting idea, but how do you persuade your colleagues of these links when everything in the system works towards increasing the separation between the two?
Many different kinds of institutions are called universities, these days. It seems to me that one feature of a university education, however, is that it involves teaching, which is *in some sense* research led. Now exactly what this means is not usually made clear. My university has a policy that teaching takes place in a research environment, and in my department we have an explicit policy that all teaching is research led. We are now in a process of exploring what this research led policy really means in practice, and a number of quite different suggestions have been made: that it is about teaching informed by the latest research; that it is a recognition that the learning process of the students is a kind of research process; that our teaching prepares students to be able to conduct research; that teaching is in some way a research process; that the commitment of the teachers to their own research informs their teaching; and yet other understandings along some of the lines suggested in Chapter 2. Perhaps it is each of these things at different times and on different courses. Unless we are able to articulate what being research led means in relation to our teaching, however,

the policy is meaningless and, worse, it can amount to no more than adherence to a myth.

Colleagues in a department may have radically opposed views and it may be difficult to arrive at a consensus policy. The process of exploring the question, and perhaps involving finding out the students' views about their teachers' involvement in research (see Breen and Lindsay 1999 for an interesting study of this), might serve not only to clarify policy but also to provide a focus for enquiry.

Spending too much time measuring and documenting everything related to teaching, just in order to meet the requirement of accountability, can be counterproductive. But I *do* believe that if I make claims like, for example, that my teaching is research led, or that it is student-centred, or that it aims to develop a critical approach, then I should be able to say what these things mean in relation to my practice of teaching and the students' experience of learning. Too often educational documentation contains terms whose meanings are assumed but rarely articulated.

Finally, I realize that my answers to your questions have not solved your difficulties but I hope that you will accept that enquiry can enable you to develop a language for articulating difficulties and uncertainties with clarity, thereby opening a door for real and lasting change.

References

Abercrombie, M. (1993) *The Human Nature of Learning: Selections from the Work of M.L.J. Abercrombie* (ed. J. Nias). Milton Keynes: Society for Research into Higher Education & Open University Press.

Abercrombie, M. and Terry, P. (1978) *Talking to Learn: Improving Teaching and Learning in Small Groups.* Guildford: Society for Research into Higher Education.

African National Congress (ANC) (1997) *Higher Education Bill, 1997.* Cape Town: Government of National Unity.

Avis, G. (1996) Survival and renewal: Developments in higher education in post-Soviet Russia, *Education in Russia, The Independent States and Eastern Europe,* 14(2): 50–64.

Barnett, R. (1990) *The Idea of Higher Education.* Milton Keynes: Society for Research into Higher Education & Open University Press.

Barnett, R. (1994) *The Limits of Competence.* Milton Keynes: Society for Research into Higher Education & Open University Press.

Barnett, R. (1997) *Higher Education: A Critical Business.* Milton Keynes: Society for Research into Higher Education & Open University Press.

Barthes, R. (1977) *Image – Music – Text* (trans. S. Heath). Glasgow: Fontana/Collins.

Barton, L. (1996) A policy statement, *Teaching and Learning in Higher Education,* 1(1): 5–6.

Beard, R. and Hartley, J. (1984) *Teaching and Learning in Higher Education,* 4th edn. London: Harper & Row.

Becher, T. (1989) *Academic Tribes and Territories.* Milton Keynes: Society for Research into Higher Education & Open University Press.

Becher, T. and Kogan, M. (1980) *Process and Structure in Higher Education.* London: Heinemann.

Blake, N., Smith, R. and Standish, P. (1998) *The Universities We Need: Higher Education after Dearing.* London: Kogan Page.

Bolton, G. (1994) Stories at work. Fictional-critical writing as a means of professional development, *British Educational Research Journal,* 20(1): 55–68.

Bolton, G. (1999) *The Therapeutic Potential of Creative Writing: Writing Myself.* London: Jessica Kingsley.

Booth, C. (1998) *Accreditation and Teaching in Higher Education.* London: Committee of Vice-chancellors and Principals of the Universities of the United Kingdom.

Boud, D., Cohen, R. and Walker, W. (eds) (1993) *Using Experience for Learning.* London: Society for Research into Higher Education & Open University Press.

Bourdieu, P.P. (1988) *Homo Academicus.* Oxford: Basil Blackwell.

Boyer, E. (1994) Scholarship reconsidered: priorities for a new century, in *The Universities in the Twenty-First Century* (a lecture series). London: The National Commission on Education.

Breen, R. and Lindsay, R. (1999) Academic research and student motivation, *Studies in Higher Education*, 24(1): 75–93.

Bridges, D. (1992) Enterprise and Liberal Education, *Journal of Philosophy of Education*, 26(1): 91–8.

Broers, A. (1999) Diversity and quality will thrive under light touch, *Times Higher Education Supplement*, 29 January, p. 10.

Calman, K. (1999) Foreword, in G. Bolton, *The Therapeutic Potential of Creative Writing: Writing Myself*, p. 9. London: Jessica Kingsley.

Carr, W. (1995) *For Education: Towards Critical Educational Inquiry.* Buckingham: Open University Press.

Carr, W. and Kemmis, S. (1986) *Becoming Critical: Education, Knowledge and Action Research.* London: Falmer Press.

Carrotte, P. (1994) An action research cycle in the teaching of restorative dentistry: how my students respond to an invitation to take control and involvement in their own learning. Unpublished MEd dissertation, University of Sheffield.

Cockburn, C. (1989) Equal opportunities: the long and short agenda, *Industrial Relations Journal*, Autumn: 213–25.

Committee of Vice-chancellors and Principals' Academic Audit Unit (1992) Letter to vice-chancellors accompanying the first annual report of the director. Birmingham: Committee of Vice-Chancellors and Principals of the United Kingdom.

Committee on Higher Education (1963) *Higher Education.* London: HMSO.

Department for Education and Employment (DfEE) (1998a) *Excellence in Research on Schools.* London: HMSO.

Department for Education and Employment (DfEE) (1998b) *Higher Education Funding for 1990–00 and Beyond.* London: HMSO.

Department of Education and Science (DES) (1991) *Primary Education: A Statement by the Secretary of State for Education and Science.* London: HMSO.

Descartes, R. (1960) *Discourse on Method and Other Writings* (trans. A. Wollaston). Harmondsworth: Penguin Books.

Dewey, J. (1939) *Freedom and Culture.* New York: Putman.

Egan, G. (1974) *The Skilled Helper: A Model for Systematic Helping and Interpersonal Relations.* Monterey, CA: Brooks/Cole.

Eisner, E.W. (1979) *The Educational Imagination: On the Design and Evaluation of School Programs.* London: Collier Macmillan.

Elton, L. and Partington, P. (1993) *Teaching Standards and Excellence in Higher Education.* Sheffield: Committee of Vice-chancellors and Principals of the Universities of the United Kingdom, Universities' and Colleges' Staff Development Unit.

Entwistle, N. (1992) *The Impact of Teaching on Learning Outcomes in Higher Education: A Literature Review.* Sheffield: Committee of Vice-chancellors and Principals of the Universities of the United Kingdom, Universities' and Colleges' Staff Development Unit.

Feyerabend, P.K. (1975) *Against Method: Outline of an Anarchistic Theory of Knowledge.* London: New Left Books.

Foucault, M. (1981) *The History of Sexuality* (vol. 1). Harmondsworth: Pelican.
Foucault, M. (1984) The ethic of care for the self as a practice of freedom, in J. Bernauer and D. Rasmussen (eds) *The Final Foucault.* Cambridge, MA: MIT Press.
Friere, P. (1972a) *Pedagogy of the Oppressed.* London: Penguin.
Friere, P. (1972b) *Cultural Action for Freedom.* London: Penguin.
Gibbs, G. and Habeshaw, S. (1987) *53 Interesting Things to Do in your Lectures,* 2nd edn. Bristol: Technical and Educational Services.
Gibran, K. (1923) *The Prophet.* London: Heinemann.
Gosling, D. (1997) Educational Development and Institutional Change in Higher Education, in K. Moti Gokulsing and C. DaCosta (eds) *Usable Knowledges as the Goal of University Education.* London: Edwin Mellen Press.
Greer, G. (1970) *The Female Eunuch.* London: MacGibbon.
Grundy, S. and Kemmis, S. (1984) Educational action research in Australia: the state of the art (an overview), in W. Flanagan, C. Breen and M. Walker (eds) *Action Research: Justified Optimism or Wishful Thinking.* Cape Town: University of Cape Town Press.
Gustad, J.W. (1966) Community, consensus and conflict, *The Educational Record,* Fall 1966, reported in Bourdieu, P. (1988).
Habermas, J. (1972) *Knowledge and Human Interests* (trans. J. Shapiro). London: Heinemann.
Habermas, J. (1974) *Theory and Practice* (trans. J. Viersal). London: Heinemann.
Habermas, J. (1984, 1987) *The Theory of Communicative Action,* vols 1 and 2 (trans. T. McCarthy). London: Heinneman.
Halsey, A.H. and Trow, M.A. (1971) *The British Academics.* London: Faber & Faber.
Hand, R. (1999) Hard questions – easy science? Or why do scientists not teach philosophy? *Teaching in Higher Education,* 4(1): 121–4.
Harré, P. and Secord, P.F. (1972) *The Explanation of Social Behaviour.* Oxford: Blackwell.
Hassan, I. (1987) *The Postmodern Turn: Essays in Postmodern Theory and Culture.* Columbus, OH: Ohio State University.
Heidegger, M. (1978) *Basic Writings* (ed. D. Krell). London: RKP.
Higher Education Funding council of England (HEFCE) (1992) *The Impact of the 1992 Research Assessment Exercise on Higher Education Institutions in England.* London: HEFCE.
Hofstadter, D. (1979) *Bach, Escher, Gödel: An Eternal Golden Braid.* London: Penguin.
Holt, J. (1965) *How Children Fail.* New York: Pitman.
Illich, I. (1970) *Deschooling Society.* London: Calder and Boyers.
Institute of Learning and Teaching (ILT) (1999) *ILT Consultation: The National Framework for Higher Education Teaching.* London: ILT.
Institute of Learning and Teaching Planning Group (ILTPG) (1998) *The Institute of Learning and Teaching: Implementing the Vision.* London: ILTPG.
Irigaray, L. (1991) *The Irigaray Reader* (ed. M. Whitford). Oxford: Blackwell.
Jacques, D. (1989) *Small Group Teaching, Module 5.* Oxford: Oxford Polytechnic.
Jenkins, A., Blackman, B., Lindsay, R. and Paton-Saltzberg, R. (1998) Teaching and research: student perpectives and policy implications, *Studies in Higher Education,* 23(2): 127–41.
Johnson, R. (1998) Student feedback as technical control. Student feedback as technology of communication. Paper presented to the Learning Technology Network Conference of the Staff Educational Development Association, Southampton, 6–8 April.

Kirpotin, S. (1999) The challenge of developing innovative teaching methods in a Russian university, *Teaching in Higher Education*, 4(3): 415–17.

Kolb, D. (1984) *Experiential Learning*. Englewood Cliffs, NJ: Prentice Hall.

Leftwich, A. (1991) Pedagogy for the depressed: the political economy of teaching development in British universities, *Studies in Higher Education*, 16(3): 277–90.

Lyotard, J-F. (1986) *The Postmodern Explained to Children*. London: Turnaround.

McWilliam, E. (1996) Touchy subjects: a risky inquiry into pedagogical pleasure, *British Educational Research Journal*, 22(3): 305–17.

Marcuse, H. (1969) *Eros and Civilisation*. London: Allen Lane.

Marton, F., Beaty, E. and Dall'Alba, G. (1993) Conceptions of learning, *International Journal of Educational Research*, 19(3): 277–300.

Marton, F., Hounsell, D.J. and Entwistle, N.J. (1997) (eds) *The Experience of Learning*, 2nd edn. Edinburgh: Scottish Academic Press.

Matthews, G. (1980) *Philosophy and the Young Child*. Cambridge, MA: Harvard University Press.

National Commission on Higher Education (NCHE) (1996) A framework for transformation – higher education system governance funding: discussion document. Pretoria: NCHE.

National Committee of Inquiry into Higher Education (NCIHE) (1997) *Higher Education in the Learning Society* (the Dearing Report). London: HMSO.

National Foundation for Educational Research (NFER) (1991) *Enterprise in Higher Education: Second Year National Evaluation*. London: NFER.

Ndaba, W.J. (1996) Teaching humanities at historically black institutions: taking African traditions seriously, *Academic Development*, 2(2): 5–17.

Ndebele, N.S. (1995) Maintaining domination through language, *Academic Development*, 1(1): 3–5.

Newman, J.H. (1976) *The Idea of a University* (ed. I.T. Ker). Oxford: Oxford University Press (first published 1853).

Pedlar, M., Boydell, T. and Burgoyne, J. (1988) *Learning Company Project Report*. Sheffield: Manpower Services Commission.

Phillips, D. (1994) Research mission and research manpower, in The National Commission on Education, *The Universities in the Twenty-First Century*. London: HMSO.

Plato (1971) *The Republic* (ed. J. Cornford). London: Penguin.

Postman, N. and Weingartner, C. (1969) *Teaching as a Subversive Activity*. New York: Delacorte Press.

Richardson, J., Eysenck, M.W. and Warren Piper, D. (1987) *Student Learning*. Milton Keynes: Society for Research into Higher Education & Open University Press.

Rogers, C.R. (1969) *Freedom to Learn: A View of What Education Might Become*. Columbus, OH: Charles E. Merrill.

Rogers, C.R. (1978) *Carl Rogers on Personal Power*. London: Constable.

Rogers, J. (1999) Research assessment exercise 2001: research into teaching, *Teaching in Higher Education*, 4(2): 285–6.

Rorty, R. (1982) *Contingency, Irony, Solidarity*. Cambridge: Cambridge University Press.

Rowan, J. (1990) *Subpersonalities: The People Inside Us*. London: Routledge.

Rowland, S. (1984) *The Enquiring Classroom*. Basingstoke: Falmer Press.

Rowland, S. (1993) *The Enquiring Tutor*. Basingstoke: Falmer Press.

Rowland, S. and Barton, L. (1994) Making things difficult: developing a research approach to teaching in higher education, *Studies in Higher Education*, 19(3): 367–74.

Rowland, S. and Skelton, A. (1998) MEd in teaching and learning for university staff: survey of course participants. Mimeo, University of Sheffield.

Russell, B. (1946) *History of Western Philosophy*. London: George Allen and Unwin.

Ruth, D. (1996) Teaching at a South African university, *Teaching in Higher Education*, 1(1): 127–33.

Sacks, O. (1985) *The Man who Mistook his Wife for a Hat*. London: Picador/Macmillan.

Schön, D. (1983) *The Reflective Practitioner*. New York: Basic Books.

Scott, P. (1984) *The Crisis of the University*. London: Croom Helm.

Smith, P.B. (1969) *Improving Skills in Working with People: The T-group*. Department of Employment and Productivity Training Information Paper 4. London: HMSO.

Stephenson, J. and Laycock, M. (1993) *Using Learning Contracts in Higher Education*. London: Kogan Page.

Stratford, J. (1999) *Learning and the Teacher's Role*. Unpublished MEd portfolio 4, University of Sheffield.

Sutherland, S. (1994) The idea of a university?, in The National Commission on Education, *The Universities in the Twenty-first Century*. London: HMSO.

Terenzini, P.T. and Pascarella, E.T. (1994) Living with myths: the undergraduate education in America, *Change*, 26(1): 28–32.

Thompson, J.B. and Held, D. (eds) (1982) *Habermas: Critical Debates*. London: Macmillan.

Tooley, J. and Darby, D. (1998) *Education Research: An Ofsted Critique*. London: Office for Standards in Education.

Valenta, Z. (1974) To see a chemist thinking, in E. Sheffield (ed.) *Teaching in the Universities: No One Way*. Montreal: McGill/Queen's University Press.

Van Manen, M. (1988) The relation between research and pedagogy, in W. Pinar (ed.) *Contemporary Curriculum Discourses*. Scotsdale, AZ: Gorsuch Scarisbrook.

Whitehead, J. (1993) *The Growth of Educational Knowledge: Creating Your Own Living Educational Theories*. Bournemouth: Hyde Publications.

Winter, R. (1991) Fictional-critical writing as a method of educational research, *British Educational Research Journal*, 17(3): 251–62.

Winter, R. and Maisch, M. (1996) *Professional Competence and Higher Education: The ASSET Programme*. London: Falmer Press.

Winter, R., Buck, A. and Sobiechowska, P. (1999) *Professional Experience and the Investigative Imagination: The ART of Reflective Writing*. London: Routledge.

Winterson, J. (1993) *Written on the Body*. London: Vintage.

Wordsworth, W. (1975) *William Wordsworth: Selected Poems*. (ed. W. Davies). London: Dent & Sons (first published 1850).

Index

The Society for Research into Higher Education

The Society for Research into Higher Education (SRHE) exists to stimulate and coordinate research into all aspects of higher education. It aims to improve the quality of higher education through the encouragement of debate and publication on issues of policy, on the organization and management of higher education institutions, and on the curriculum, teaching and learning methods.

The Society is entirely independent and receives no subsidies, although individual events often receive sponsorship from business or industry. The Society is financed through corporate and individual subscriptions and has members from many parts of the world.

Under the imprint *SRHE & Open University Press*, the Society is a specialist publisher of research, having over 80 titles in print. In addition to *SRHE News*, the Society's newsletter, the Society publishes three journals: *Studies in Higher Education* (three issues a year), *Higher Education Quarterly* and *Research into Higher Education Abstracts* (three issues a year).

The Society runs frequent conferences, consultations, seminars and other events. The annual conference in December is organized at and with a higher education institution. There are a growing number of networks which focus on particular areas of interest, including:

Access
Assessment
Consultants
Curriculum Development
Eastern European
Educational Development Research
FE/HE
Funding
Graduate Employment

Learning Environment
Legal Education
Managing Innovation
New Technology for Learning
Postgraduate Issues
Quantitative Studies
Student Development
Vocational Qualifications

Benefits to members

Individual

- The opportunity to participate in the Society's networks
- Reduced rates for the annual conferences

- Free copies of *Research into Higher Education Abstracts*
- Reduced rates for *Studies in Higher Education*
- Reduced rates for *Higher Education Quarterly*
- Free copy of *Register of Members' Research Interests* – includes valuable reference material on research being pursued by the Society's members
- Free copy of occasional in-house publications, e.g. *The Thirtieth Anniversary Seminars Presented by the Vice-Presidents*
- Free copies of *SRHE News* which informs members of the Society's activities and provides a calendar of events, with additional material provided in regular mailings
- A 35 per cent discount on all SRHE/Open University Press books
- Access to HESA statistics for student members
- The opportunity for you to apply for the annual research grants
- Inclusion of your research in the *Register of Members' Research Interests*

Corporate

- Reduced rates for the annual conferences
- The opportunity for members of the Institution to attend SRHE's network events at reduced rates
- Free copies of *Research into Higher Education Abstracts*
- Free copies of *Studies in Higher Education*
- Free copies of *Register of Members' Research Interests* – includes valuable reference material on research being pursued by the Society's members
- Free copy of occasional in-house publications
- Free copies of *SRHE News*
- A 35 per cent discount on all SRHE/Open University Press books
- Access to HESA statistics for research for students of the Institution
- The opportunity for members of the Institution to submit applications for the Society's research grants
- The opportunity to work with the Society and co-host conference
- The opportunity to include in the *Register of Members' Research Interests* your Institution's research into aspects of higher education

Membership details: SRHE, 3 Devonshire Street, London W1N 2BA, UK. Tel: 020 7637 2766. Fax: 020 7637 2781. email: srhe@mailbox.ulcc.ac.uk
world wide web: http://www.srhe.ac.uk/srhe/
Catalogue: SRHE & Open University Press, Celtic Court, 22 Ballmoor, Buckingham MK18 1XW. Tel: 01280 823388. Fax: 01280 823233. email: enquiries@openup.co.uk